FROM STONEHENGE TO BREXIT

A BRIEF SURVEY OF BRITISH HISTORY

TOM BLISS

FROM STONEHENGE TO BREXIT

Other Works by the same author

BLISSFUL TIMES: The Bliss Families of Eastern England, Spindthrift Print & Publishing 1997. ISBN09530902 05

To John.

Thanks for your help old Pal Tried

Tom.

FROM STONEHENGE TO BREXIT

I gratefully acknowledge the help received from John Perkins who assiduously proof-read my original notes and made many useful contributions to the following timeline of events and personalities.

CONTENTS

FROM STONEHENGE TO BREXIT

FROM STONEHENGE TO BREXIT

1. Introduction

Nobody can truly begin to understand a nation if they don't have a working knowledge of the people and events from the past which shaped the destiny of that country. This book is intended to be an aid for comprehending the broad sweep and depth of British history and to assist those who wish to learn something about the development of Britain, its culture, customs and practices and its various national qualities. It is a catalogue of national achievements and failures, of famous or infamous events and people, of notable inventions and discoveries, of social and leisure developments, and of literary and artistic creativity.

However, nobody should look here for complete information on any person or subject. This book merely itemises inform-ation and places it in a historical context; many of the people and events mentioned are subjects of continuing discussion and this synopsis tries not to promote or belittle anything or anyone, leaving it up to the reader to consult other sources for further information about those matters.

Some things listed here may seem insignificant or unremark-able today but they all once had importance and helped shape our national story and/or influenced our place in the world. Inevitably, there are many significant omissions from the vast parade of a nation's history covering such a long span of time, but the contents are designed to give a fair idea of the way our peoples developed into a nation over the ages and made their way in the wider world.

There will inevitably be those who complain that the record is Anglo-centric, although I have done my best to pay tribute to people and events in Wales, Ireland, Scotland and elsewhere which have contributed to British history. It is hoped that this little work will benefit those who wish to begin the journey of discovery about how the United Kingdom and its people came into being and how we have arrived at this present stage in our development.

I hope those who may have grown up in the UK with an imperfect historical knowledge of these islands and those who have arrived here to make a new life here will find enough in these pages to give them a more rounded know-ledge of the United Kingdom and its culture. Should anyone feel after consulting these pages that they have a better understanding of what it means to be British and a better sense of the continuity from our ancient past to the present, the author considers the effort spent putting this timeline together was worthwhile.

Tom Bliss

2. Prehistory BCE 6500 and the Roman Era to 410

Pre-history

Circa 6,500 BCE   The British Isles are separated from the European mainland by the English Channel.

Circa 3,500 BCE   A Neolithic culture based on agriculture develops, leaving long barrows and hilltop enclosures such as Maiden Castle as evidence.

Circa 2,500 BCE   Henge monuments, including Stonehenge, become widespread throughout Britain.

Circa 1,500 BCE   Bronze Age cultures develop with round barrows containing cremated remains and refined metal-working techniques.
        Fenland settlements become established.

Circa 500 BCE   Celtic culture arrives from the continent with iron weapons and implements.

Circa 330-320 BCE   Pytheas of Massilia (Marseilles), a Greek explorer, circumnavigates Britain and writes about the Cornish tin trade with the Mediterranean.

The Roman Era

54 BCE Julius Caesar mounts a full scale raid on Britain (known as Britannia) but returns to Gaul.

43 AD   The Emperor Claudius captures Colchester and Britannia becomes a Roman province.

61 AD   Boudicca leads the Iceni rebellion against Romans. Colchester is burnt and London is sacked.

122 AD The Emperor Hadrian builds a wall as a boundary between Britannia and the Scots and Picts to the North.

Circa 215 AD Britannia is reorganised into two provinces by the Emperor Caracalla.

250 AD Early Christians are persecuted by the Emperor Severus- execution of St Alban, Britain's first Christian martyr?

286-296 AD Britannia is held by rebel Roman forces led by Carausius until reclaimed by Constantius (who was later declared Emperor).

306 AD Constantine the Great is declared Emperor at York.

314 AD Three British bishops (York, London and Lincoln?) attend the Council of Arles.

388 AD Last Roman coinage is minted in Britannia (Emperor Maximus).

410 AD The Legions are withdrawn; Britannia is abandoned by the Roman Emperor Honorius.

3. The Anglo-Saxon/ Viking period 430 – 1066

430   Pagan immigrants, Saxons supposedly led by Hengist and Horsa, begin to settle in Kent as 'protectors' of the (Romano-Celtic) British.

447-50   Angles, Saxons, Jutes and Frieslanders join the earlier settlers in the south and begin the wholesale colonisation of eastern and southern Britain. They eventually form several small kingdoms but become collectively known as the Anglelanders or English.

461   The traditional date for the death of St Patrick, patron saint and missionary who brought Christianity to Ireland from his Romano-British homeland.

470-500 British natives, mainly Christian, are driven west into Wales, Cornwall and the North West by the pagan English.

516   Possible date of the Battle of Mount Badon where the British King Arthur supposedly defeated the English under king Aelle of Sussex.

563   St Columba from Ireland establishes a monastery at Iona, the main centre of the Celtic Christian church in Britain.

597   Pope Gregory I sends St Augustine, first Archbishop of Canterbury, to begin the conversion of the southern English.

616   The first English laws are issued by King Ethelbert of Kent.

Circa 624 Death of Raedwald, King of the East Angles, probably buried in the ship burial uncovered in 1939 at Sutton Hoo, Suffolk.

634   St Aidan from Iona establishes a Celtic monastery at the isle of Lindisfarne in the Anglian kingdom of Northumbria.

655   King Penda of Mercia is slain at battle of the Winwaed and Mercia becomes Christianised.

664   The Synod of Whitby settles disputes between the Roman and Celtic churches. Rome's supremacy is recognised.

685   The Picts defeat King Ecgfrith of Northumbria at the battle of Dun Nechtain, freeing much of Scotland from its Anglian overlords.

731   The Venerable Bede, a monk at Jarrow monastery, Northumbria, completes the Ecclesiastical History of The English.

784   Offa, King of Mercia builds his dyke to define the English-Welsh/British border.

793   The Viking raids begin. Vikings (Danes/Norwegians) attack Lindisfarne.

802   Vikings attack Iona in Scotland.

838   The battle of Hingston Down. Cornwall becomes a vassal state of the king of Wessex.
       Vikings establish a settlement on the river Liffey in Ireland which develops into Dublin.

843   Kenneth MacAlpin becomes the first King of the Scots and Picts.

866   Vikings capture York.

869   Danes kill St Edmund, the martyr king of East Anglia.

875   Orkney and Shetland are taken by the King of Norway.

878   King Alfred the Great of Wessex defeats the Danes at the battle of Edington.
British kings in South Wales recognise King Alfred as their overlord.

886   The Danelaw is established in Eastern England, a large part of which is dominated by the Danes. English residents are equal under the Danish law.

892   The Anglo Saxon Chronicles, historical annals written in Old English, begin to be distributed around churches.

902   Norsemen begin to colonise North West Britain.

927   Athelstan, Alfred's grandson and King of Wessex and Mercia, becomes King of the English.

980   Danish raids are renewed and widespread settlements are established in Eastern England.

991   Danes win the Battle of Maldon against Ethelred the Unready who pays a £10,000 tribute known as Danegeld.

997   King Ethelred introduces the Law Code of Wantage, including the Danish custom of trial by jury of twelve.

1002   The St Brice's Day massacre of Danes in England results in renewed Danish invasions.

1016   The Danish King Cnut becomes King of all England.

1040   Macbeth kills Duncan and becomes King of the Scots.

1042   Edward the Confessor is elected king in succession to the Danish kings.

4. The Norman-French Ascendancy 1066 – 1400

1066   The Battle of Hastings. Death of the last Anglo-Saxon king Harold II, and the overthrow of the English ruling class by William the Conqueror of Normandy.

1086   Domesday Book. A taxation survey of all England's assets and people. Earliest surviving Norman-English national public record.

1100   King William II (nicknamed Rufus) dies, being shot by an arrow while hunting in the New Forest.
          Henry I is crowned and issues a Coronation Charter declaring the traditional laws of Edward the Confessor will be restored.

1154   End of the Great Anarchy caused by civil war between The supporters of King Stephen and the Empress Matilda, the daughter of Henry I.
          Henry II, Matilda's son, becomes the first Plantagenet king.

1155   Adrian IV (the only English pope) issues the papal bull *Laudabiliter* which encourages an invasion of Ireland by Henry II to bring the Celtic church under papal control.

1170   Murder of Thomas Becket, Archbishop of Canterbury, by knights loyal to Henry II, with whom Becket has quarrelled over attempts to make priests liable to trial in royal courts.

1171   Henry II is acknowledged by Irish princes as the Lord of Ireland.

1174   The Treaty of Falaise - William the Lion, King of Scots recognises Henry II as his overlord.

1191   Richard I, the Lionheart, fails to recapture Jerusalem on the 3rd Crusade.

1193   Heavy taxes are raised by Prince John to pay a ransom for his brother Richard I, taken prisoner in Austria whilst returning from the 3rd Crusade.

1209   Scholars depart the schools at Oxford and found a second English university at Cambridge.

1214   The battle of Bouvines in Flanders. The King of France destroys an allied army intent on taking back territory he has captured. This finishes King John's hopes of regaining Normandy and most of his other lands in France.

1215   King John issues Magna Carta, regarded as the foundation of English liberty from arbitrary rule by the crown.

1258   The Provisions of Oxford, the first government document written in English since the Conquest.
        Henry III is obliged by barons led by Simon de Montfort to appoint Privy Council overseers, monitored by regular meetings of Parliament, to supervise his administration.

1265   Simon de Montfort calls the first representative Parliament to which elected members are returned from selected boroughs.
        Lord Edward (later Edward I) defeats de Montfort and the Reform Party at the Battle of Evesham.

1283   Llewelyn ap Gruffudd, Prince of Wales, is killed and Wales is subjugated by Edward I's huge castle building programme at Conwy, Caernarfon etc.

1290   Edward I expels the Jews from England.

1292-4 An interregnum in Scotland. Scottish lords recognise Edward I of England as their overlord and invite him to adjudicate claims to the Scottish throne.

1296   Edward I claims the Scottish crown for himself. Wars with Scotland begin.

1301   Edward I's eldest son is invested as Prince of Wales.

1305   William Wallace, leader of the Scots is executed in London.

1306   Robert the Bruce is crowned King of the Scots at Scone.

1314   The Battle of Bannockburn. Robert the Bruce defeats Edward II.

1320   The Declaration of Arbroath declares Scotland to be an independent, sovereign state.

1327   Edward II is deposed by Queen Isabella and her lover Roger Mortimer and is later murdered at Berkeley Castle.

1337   The Beginning of the Hundred Years' War. Edward III lays claim to the French throne.
          Flemish weavers are invited to set up business in England. Beginning of the switch from export of English wool to manufacture of cloth for export, England's major product.

1346   The Battle of Crecy begins a series of English victories in France.

1348   The Most Noble Order of the Garter is instituted by Edward III.

1349   The Black Death. An estimated one third of the British population dies in a devastating outbreak of bubonic plague.

1351   Statute of Labourers attempts to fix wages at pre-Black Death levels and restrict the movement of labourers.

1356   Edward the Black Prince takes King John II of France, his son and many French aristocrats prisoner at the battle of Poitiers.

1371   Robert II takes the Scottish crown for the House of Stewart or Stuart, beginning periods of weak government and feuding with an intractable nobility.

1377   The first recorded mention of the Robin Hood legend in the Sloane manuscripts at the British Museum.

1380 approx. Piers Plowman, a poem by William Langland, is written in unrhymed, alliterative, Middle English verse.

1381   The Peasants' Revolt, led by Wat Tyler and John Ball, signals the breakup of the feudal system of villeins tied to the manor and holding land in return for services to their landlord.

1384   Lollards, the followers of John Wyclif, demand reforms of the Church.

1387   Geoffrey Chaucer begins writing the Canterbury Tales, demonstrating the final ascendancy of the evolved English language over Latin and Norman French.

5. The Lancastrian and Yorkist Interlude 1400 -1485

1400   King Richard II is deposed by his cousin Henry Boling-broke, Duke of Lancaster. End of the Plantagenet dynasty.

1412   The last recorded sighting of Owain Glyndwr, leader of a final major Welsh revolt.

1415   Henry V defeats the French at Agincourt and is recognised by the French king as his heir.

1432   Joan of Arc is burnt at stake but has inspired French resistance. France begins to slip from English control.

1453   End of the Hundred Years War. All English claims to property in France are lost except for Calais.

1455   The First Battle of St Albans begins the Wars of the Roses between York and Lancaster claimants to the English crown due to the mental instability of King Henry VI.

1461   The battle of Towton Moor. Edward of York defeats the Lancastrians and assumes the crown.

1471   The battle of Tewkesbury ends the Lancastrian royal line. Edward, Prince of Wales is killed and his father King Henry VI was put to death soon after.

1472   Scotland annexes the isles of Orkney and Shetland.

1477   William Caxton sets up England's first printing press.

1483   Edward IV dies and his children are declared illeg-itimate by his brother Richard of Gloucester.
      The Princes in the Tower disappear. Their uncle is crowned King Richard III.

1485   Richard III is defeated at the battle of Bosworth.
Henry Tudor becomes Henry VII, marries Elizabeth of York,
sister of the lost princes, and founds the new Tudor dynasty.

6. The Tudors 1485 – 1603

1489   Coinage Reform. The first gold sovereign is minted.

1492   John Cabot sails from Bristol and begins the English exploration of the North American coast.

1501   Arthur Prince of Wales dies, succeeded by his brother Henry who also married his widow Katherine of Aragon.

1513   An invading Scots army is routed at the battle of Flodden and King James IV is killed.

1526   William Tyndale begins to publish the Bible in vernacular English - an illegal act for which he is later burnt.

1533   Henry VIII's marriage to Katherine of Aragon is declared void despite papal objections. The king is excommunicated by the Pope and marries Ann Boleyn.

1534   The Act of Supremacy confirms Henry VIII as Supreme Governor of the Church of England.

1535   Thomas More, recently Lord Chancellor, is executed for treason.

1536-9 Dissolution of the Monasteries. Reformation of the Church is imposed in England.

1540   Thomas Cromwell, the king's first minister and leader of Church reform, is executed.

1543   Consolidating Act of Welsh Union. 12 counties and the Council of Wales are established.

1549   The English Book of Common Prayer is introduced. It remains the Christian liturgy of over fifty countries in the world.

1553   The Accession of Mary I, daughter of Henry VIII and Katherine of Aragon.
        Roman worship is restored to English churches and Protestant Marian Martyrs are burnt.

1554   Lady Jane Grey 'The 9 Day Queen', protestant pretender to the throne, is executed.
        Mary I marries Philip, the heir to the Spanish crown and became queen consort when he becomes king of Spain in 1556.

1558   Calais, the last English possession in France is lost.
        Queen Mary I dies childless succeeded by her half-sister Elizabeth I, daughter of Henry VIII and Ann Boleyn.

1559   The Act of Supremacy restores the anti-papacy laws and restores the queen as head of the English church.
        John Knox leads the Scottish Reformation and over-throws Mary of Guise's regency on behalf of her daughter Mary, Queen of Scots.

1562-4 Sir John Hawkins begins the English trans-Atlantic slave trade, taking slaves from Africa to Hispaniola, a Spanish colony in the Caribbean, and introduces tobacco to England.

1567   Mary Queen of Scots goes into exile in England.

1571   The Royal Exchange, founded by Thomas Gresham, opens as a centre for commerce in the City of London.

1580   Sir Francis Drake arrives in London after sailing round the world in the Golden Hind.

1583   Newfoundland, seasonally visited by European fisher-men, is claimed as England's first colony by Sir Humphrey Gilbert but no permanent settlement is established.

1585   Sir Walter Raleigh attempts to establish a colony at Roanoke in North America.

1587   Mary Queen of Scots is executed for treason against Elizabeth I.

1588   The Spanish Armada is defeated. England is saved from invasion.

1590   The First Shakespeare plays are produced - Henry VI part I and Titus Andronicus.

1591   Sir Richard Grenville, commanding the queen's ship The Revenge, dies of wounds after fighting a Spanish squadron single handed for 15 hours at Flores in the Azores.

1597   The Poor Relief Act. Local rates are to support relief of the poor and parish workhouses to house the old and infirm.

1600   The East India Company is chartered.

1601   Poor Relief Act refines the 1597 Act and forms the basis of support for the poor and infirm based on the parish for the next two centuries.

1603   Elizabeth I dies. The end of the Tudor dynasty.
        The accession of James VI, son of Mary Queen of Scots, to the English throne as James I.

7. The Stuart, Commonwealth and Restoration Years to the Glorious Revolution 1603 – 1688

1605   Discovery of the Catholic Gunpowder Plot to blow up king and parliament. Guy Fawkes is arrested and executed with other plotters.

1606   The first Union Flag amalgamates the flag of St George of England and the Scottish St Andrew's saltire.

1607   John Smith founds a colonial settlement at Jamestown in America on behalf of the Virginia Company.

1609   The Plantation of Ulster begins. English and Scots Protestants are settled on the forfeited estates of rebel Irish earls.
       The Virginia Company begins the permanent settlement of Bermuda.

1610   Sir Edward Coke, Chief Justice of the Court of Common Pleas, rules that the king has no prerogative but that which the law of the land allows.

1611   The Authorised version of The Bible is published.

1616   The death of Shakespeare, Britain's foremost playwright and poet.

1618   The English West Africa Company begins trading with Gambia and the Gold Coast.

1619   William Harvey proposes the theory of the circulation of the blood.

1620   The Pilgrim Fathers sail aboard the Mayflower to establish the Plymouth colony in New England.
1621   The Commons Protestation defending Parliamentary privilege is rejected by the king.

1623   The First Folio of Shakespeare's plays is published seven years after his death.

1625   Barbados is claimed as the first English Caribbean colony.

1628   The Petition of Right curtails the royal prerogative and recognises rights and privileges of people which the king is not permitted to infringe.

1636   John Hampden refuses to pay Ship Money, levied by Charles I without parliamentary consent on London and coastal towns and later extended to inland towns.

1638   The National Covenant in support of Presbyterianism circulates in Scotland. Scots Covenanters take up arms against the king.

1640   The Star Chamber, a court renowned for arbitrary and abusive procedures, is abolished.
        Habeas Corpus Act allows writs to be issued requiring prisoners to be brought before a court. It is reissued in 1679.

1642   Charles I, accompanied by soldiers, enters the House of Commons but fails to arrest the Five Members he seeks to apprehend.
        Charles raises his standard at Nottingham. The English Civil War begins.

1643   Parliament's 'Roundhead' forces ally with the Scottish Covenanters' Army against the King.

1645   The battle of Naseby. The parliamentary New Model Army under Oliver Cromwell and Sir Thomas Fairfax destroys the royalist army.

1646   Charles I surrenders to the Scots Covenanters' army which deliver him to the English Parliamentarians.

1647   The Putney Debates. Factions within the New Model Army, including the Levellers, consider proposals for democracy and a new constitution for England.

1648   A second Civil War briefly flares as royalist, presbyterian parliamentarians and Scots sympathisers join forces unsuccessfully against the New Model Army.
        Cromwell defeats a Scots and royalist army at the battle of Preston.
        Colonel Pride purges presbyterian Members of Parliament who support a settlement with the king.

1649   Charles I is beheaded. The monarchy and House of Lords are abolished. England is proclaimed to be 'A Commonwealth'.
        Charles II is proclaimed King of Scotland.
        The Battle of Dunbar. Cromwell defeats a Scottish army loyal to Charles II.
        Cromwell puts down a pro-royalist Catholic rebellion in Ireland. Massacre at Drogheda.

1651   The Battle of Worcester. Royalists again defeated and Charles II escapes capture by hiding in an oak tree.

1652   Latin is replaced by English in legal proceedings.

1653   Cromwell becomes the Lord Protector and, backed by armed soldiers, dismisses the Rump Parliament.

1655   The Jews are allowed back into England.
Santiago in the Caribbean Sea is taken from Spain and renamed Jamaica.

1658   Oliver Cromwell dies.

1660   Restoration of the monarchy. Charles II returns to London.
Foundation of the Royal Society for the Improvement of Natural Knowledge.
The Navigation Acts, designed to promote self-sufficiency in the British Empire, restrict trade between English territories to English ships.

1664   New Amsterdam is taken by treaty from the Dutch and is renamed New York.

1665   The Great Plague of London. 70,000 deaths.

1666   The Great Fire of London. The old city is largely destroyed.

1667   John Milton's Paradise Lost is published.

1669   Samuel Pepys stops writing the diary he has kept going since Jan. 1st 1660.

1672   The Royal African Company is founded with monopoly rights to trade slaves, gold, tropical wood, etc. in English possessions at home and abroad.

1674   The Theatre Royal opens in Drury Lane.

1675   Founding of the new St Paul's cathedral, designed by Sir Christopher Wren.

1679   The terms Whig and Tory, later used to identify political parties, are first used as terms of abuse in a parliamentary debate about excluding James, Duke of York from succession to the throne.

Thomas Hobbes, English philosopher and creator of the Social Contract theory, dies.

Habeas Corpus, requiring prisoners to be brought before a court, is reissued.

1685   James II, a practising Catholic, succeeds his brother Charles II on the throne.

The Battle of Sedgemoor – protestant rebels are defeated.

1685   Judge Jeffreys condemns many rebels to death at the Bloody Assizes.

Elizabeth Gaunt is the last woman to be burnt to death for a political offence in England (see 1789).

Huguenot protestant refugees start to arrive in England following revocation of the Edict of Nantes in France.

1687   The Publication of Philosophiae Naturalis Principia Mathematica by Isaac Newton, expounding some of the founding principles of modern Physics.

1688   James II is exiled. His son in law William of Orange is invited to 'defend English liberties'.

8. Years of Expansion and Development 1689 -1772

1689   Accession of William III and Mary II.
        The Glorious Revolution: The Bill of Rights forbids
Catholics becoming monarch or consort and increases
parliamentary powers.

1690   James II and Catholic supporters are defeated at the
Battle of the Boyne in Ireland.
        The East India Company makes a treaty with the
Moghul emperor which establishes a trading post at Calcutta.
        Lloyds coffee house becomes the centre for marine
insurance business in London.

1692   The Glencoe Massacre - a portion of the clan Mac-
Donald is slaughtered by Robert Campbell's loyalist troops.

1694   The Bank of England is founded and issues £1.2
million of government 'gilt-edged' securities to fund the war
with France.

1695   Parliament refuses to renew an act requiring a licence
to print – the beginning of press freedom.
        The death of Henry Purcell, composer of sacred and
courtly baroque music and opera.

1698   Thomas Savery patents the first inefficient pistonless
steam engine.
        Failed attempt to found a Scottish colony in the
Isthmus of Darien, Central America.

1700   William Dampier explores the North West coast of
Australia.

1701   Grand Alliance of Britain, Holland and the Hapsburg emperor is formed to prevent the attempt by Louis XIV to unite the crowns of France and Spain.

1702   John Locke, pre-Enlightenment philosopher and 'Father of Liberalism', dies.

1704   The Battle of Blenheim - first of John Churchill, Duke of Marlborough's Grand alliance victories against France.
        Gibraltar is captured and becomes British in 1713 at the treaty of Utrecht.

1707   Acts of Union unite England and Scotland in the Kingdom of Great Britain governed by a single parliament at Westminster.

1709   Abraham Darby uses coke instead of charcoal to smelt iron at Coalbrookdale. Early use of coal for industrial processes.

1711   Richard Steele and Joseph Addison publish the Spectator, a literary and satirical periodical.

1712   Thomas Newcomen creates the atmospheric steam engine for pumping floodwater out of mines.

1714   The Death of Queen Anne, the last of the Stuart monarchs.
        George Ludwig of Hanover takes the throne as George I, Britain's first Hanoverian ruler.

1715   The First Jacobite Rebellion in Scotland in support of the 'Old Pretender' is put down.

1719   Robinson Crusoe, a novel by Daniel Defoe is published.

1720   The South Sea Bubble, involving corruption and speculation in Government debt, ruins many investors and damages the national economy.

1721   Sir Robert Walpole is established as Britain's first Prime minister.

1726   Gulliver's Travels by Jonathan Swift is published (amended 1735).

1729   Charles and John Wesley found the Holy club at Oxford – forerunner of the Methodist religious movement.

1732   The Theatre Royal, Covent Garden opens.

1733   Jethro Tull's Horse-Hoeing Husbandry is published – it summarises recent improvements in arable husbandry.

1739   Dick Turpin the highwayman is hanged at York.
        A Royal Charter is granted to Thomas Coram for the Foundling Hospital, a home for abandoned children later established in Bloomsbury.

1741   The London debut of acclaimed actor David Garrick as Shakespeare's Richard III.

1743   Handel's Messiah is performed at the Theatre Royal, Covent Garden – George II stands for the Hallelujah Chorus.
        Jack Broughton codifies the rules of Boxing.

1744   The first known rules of Golf are written for a competition at Leith, Scotland.

1745   The first rules of Cricket are printed.
        The Second Jacobite rebellion. Bonny Prince Charlie, the Young Pretender, advances out of Scotland to Derby but...

1746   The Jacobites are defeated at Culloden. The Duke of Cumberland, the Butcher, crushes dissent in the Highlands of Scotland.

1749   Henry Fielding creates the Bow Street Runners, Britain's first law enforcement force.

1750   The Jockey Club is founded.

1752   Great Britain abandons the 'old style' Julian calendar and 'loses' 11 days when the Gregorian calendar is adopted.

1753   The Foundation charter for the British Museum is published.

1754   The Society for Encouragement of Arts, Manufacture and Commerce is founded (later known as the Royal Society for Arts or RSA).

1755   Dr Samuel Johnson publishes the first English language dictionary.

1756   War with France - Seven Years' War or the first world-wide war.
        120 British captives of Suraj ud Dowla, the French ally in India, die in the Black Hole of Calcutta.

1757   Robert Clive defeats Suraj ud Dowla with East India Company forces in Bengal at the battle of Plassey.

1759   General James Wolfe dies at the capture of Quebec, the French capital city in Canada.
        Joseph Harrison completes H4, the first successful seagoing chronometer.

1761   James Brindley completes the Worsley to Manchester canal which reduces cost of coal to factories and mills.

1762   Buckingham Palace becomes a royal residence when George III buys it for Queen Charlotte and their children.

1764   James Hargreaves invents the Spinning Jenny - the beginning of mechanised textile production.
        William Hogarth, painter, engraver and cartoonist (The Rakes Progress etc.) dies.

1768   Captain James Cook sets off on the first of his three voyages of exploration – he explores the New Zealand coasts and lands at Botany Bay, Australia.
        The Royal Academy of Arts is founded – Sir Joshua Reynolds is its first president.

1769   The Industrial Revolution gathers pace. James Watt patents improvements to the steam engine with a separate condenser and later with rotary movement.
        Josiah Wedgewood opens the Etruria Pottery.

1770   The Deserted Village by Oliver Goldsmith, a poem critical of rural depopulation, is published.

1771   Richard Arkwright and partners begin factory mass-production of cotton thread using water power at Cromford, Derbyshire.
        Eclipse, the ancestor to most modern Thoroughbred horses, is retired to stud after an undefeated racing career.

1772   Lord Chief Justice Mansfield rules slavery cannot exist in England at the conclusion of the 'Somerset case' brought to court by Granville Sharpe.

9. The Revolutionary Age 1773 – 1815

1773   The Boston Tea Party. American colonists protest at taxation without representation.

1776   The Declaration of Independence by the American colonies.
    Adam Smith, Scottish economist, publishes The Wealth of Nations, 'the capitalist bible'.
    David Hume, Scottish philosopher and essayist dies.

1780   The Gordon Riots. Violent anti-Catholic protest in London – Parliament and Bank of England are attacked, Newgate prison is largely destroyed by 'king mob'.
    Sir Charles Bunbury's Diomed wins the first Epsom Derby Race.

1781   Earl Cornwallis surrenders at Yorktown. The American colonies are lost.
    The first bridge built of cast iron made by Abraham Darby III opens at Ironbridge in the Severn Gorge.

1783   Robert Bakewell, agriculturalist, forms the Dishley Society to promote his animal husbandry and breeding methods.
    The Treaty of Paris: recognition of the United States of America.

1784   The India Act gives the government control of the East India Company. Warren Hastings becomes first Governor General of India.
    John Wesley forms the Methodist Conference.

1785   Edmund Cartwright invents the powered loom – steam-powered textile production increases Britain's superior industrial productivity.

1787   The Society for Abolition of the Slave Trade is founded with Granville Sharpe chairman.

Attempt is made to settle freed black American loyalists in Sierra Leone, West Africa.

Marylebone Cricket Club (the MCC) is founded.

1788   The Times newspaper is named (formerly the Daily Universal Register).

Convicts on the First Fleet arrive at Botany Bay, the first penal settlement in Australia.

Thomas Gainsborough, outstanding landscape and portrait painter, dies.

1789   Natural History and Antiquities of Selborne by the rev. Gilbert White is published.

Mutiny on the Bounty. Lieutenant (later Captain) William Bligh is cast adrift, navigates more than 4000 miles to safety in the South Pacific. Mutineers settle on Pitcairn Island.

Catherine Murphy, convicted for coining, is the last woman to be burnt at the stake in Britain (at Newgate).

1790   Edmund Burke publishes Reflections on the Revolution in France.

1791   The Rights of Man is published by Thomas Paine.

The Ordnance Survey begins to map southern England using triangulation methods pioneered by William Roy.

1792   In Vindication of the Rights of Woman by Mary Wollstonecraft is published.

Sir Joshua Reynolds, fashionable portrait painter, dies.

1793   Revolutionary France declares war on Great Britain.

James Weatherby produces the General Stud book which records the pedigree of Thoroughbred horses in Great Britain and Ireland.

1795   Ceylon (Sri Lanka) is taken from Holland which has become a dependency of France.

Mungo Park, Scottish explorer, begins his exploration of the river Niger and the interior of West Africa.

Bad harvests and the increasing price of bread cause magistrates at Speenhamland, Berkshire. to introduce supplementary payments to labourers funded by local ratepayers.

1796   Edward Jenner discovers a vaccine against Smallpox.

Robert (Rabbie) Burns, national poet of Scotland, dies.

1798   Rebellion by the non-sectarian United Irishmen, seeking independence for Ireland. Its leader Wolfe Tone is captured and eludes execution by cutting his own throat.

William Wordsworth and Samuel Taylor Coleridge launch the Romantic Movement with the publication of Lyric Ballads.

1799   The repressive Combination Act bans meetings and societies interfering with commerce and trade and demanding political reform.

1800   Irish and Westminster parliaments pass Acts to form the United Kingdom of Great Britain and Ireland with one government and parliament at Westminster.

Robert Owen takes over management of New Lanark Mills in Scotland and begins a comprehensive programme of enlightened social measures for workers and their families.

The Royal Institution for encouraging applied sciences is founded.

1801   The First UK Census (8.3 million England, 2.1 million Scotland/Wales 5.2 Ireland).

1802   Major William Lambton begins the Great Trigonometrical Survey of India with a baseline measured near Madras.

The Health & Morals of Apprentices Act is designed to improve conditions for apprentices working in cotton mills with a maximum 12 hour day (excluding meal breaks).
1802   cont. William Cobbett, radical writer and politician, begins publication of the Weekly Political Register.

1803   War with France (now under the consulate of Napoleon Bonaparte) is resumed.

1804   Richard Trevithick demonstrates a train carrying a 10 ton payload propelled on rails by a steam locomotive at Pen y Darren ironworks, South Wales.

1805   Battle of Trafalgar - Admiral Lord Nelson (who lost his life in the battle) establishes supremacy of the Royal Navy on the seas and ends Bonaparte's invasion plans.

1806   The Dutch colony at the Cape of Good Hope is seized.

1807   The Slave Trade in all British possessions is abolished following a campaign by the Society for Abolition of the Slave Trade led by Granville Sharp, William Wilberforce and Thomas Clarkson.

1808   The Royal Navy West Africa Squadron is set up to suppress the Atlantic slave trade (continuous operations to 1860 free 150,000 Africans and capture 1600 slave ships).
        Jerusalem, inspirational hymn by the poet William Blake is printed and published.

1811   Luddite outbreak in Nottingham – industrial machines are broken by artisan framework knitters.
        N. M. Rothschild and Sons bank is established in London by a Jewish family from Frankfurt, Germany.

1812   Spencer Perceval is shot and killed - the only prime minister to be assassinated.

1814   Arthur Wellesley (to become the Duke of Wellington) completes the defeat of French armies in the Iberian Peninsula and enters France.

The Treaty of Paris ends the French wars.

Thomas Lord establishes his third and final cricket ground at Lords, the 'home of cricket' in St John's Wood, London.

Edmund Kean performs Shakespeare's Shylock at Drury Lane to enormous acclaim.

1815   Bonaparte returns from exile and is defeated at Waterloo by an allied army commanded by the Duke of Wellington. Britain imprisons Bonaparte on St Helena in the South Atlantic.

Corn Laws are passed to protect the price of grain - leads to unrest over the price of bread.

10. Reaction and Reform 1816 -1836

1816   The Elgin marbles, stripped from the Parthenon in Athens, are sold to the British Museum by Lord Elgin.
        Mary Wollstonecraft Shelley, women's rights radical and novelist, wife of Percy Bysshe Shelley, the poet, writes the novel Frankenstein at Geneva.

1817   Jane Austen, a seminal female novelist, dies.
        Elizabeth Fry, Quaker and humanitarian, argues for improving conditions for women prisoners in Newgate.

1818   Gas lights are introduced at Covent Garden and Brighton Pavilion.

1819   The 'Peterloo' Massacre - yeomanry shoot dead 11 people in a crowd demanding political reform at Manchester.
        Stamford Raffles founds the Singapore settlement.

1820   The Cato Street Conspirators plot to blow up the cabinet – 5 are executed, the last to be judicially beheaded in Britain.

1823   Sir Robert Peel abolishes the death penalty for more than 100 offences.
        William Huskisson's Warehousing of Goods Act begins moves for Free Trade.

1824   Repeal of the Combination Acts which banned workers' union organisations.
        Lord Byron, scandalous socialite and poet dies at Missolonghi, modern Greece.
        George IV supports purchase of the Angerstein collection to found the National Gallery.

1825   George Stevenson, 'father of railways' completes the world's first passenger-carrying steam locomotive railway line which carries 450 persons at speeds up to 15 mph from Stockton to Darlington.

1826   University College, offering non-sectarian education, is founded in London.

1828   The Spectator magazine is published (revival of a title first used in 1711).

1829   The Roman Catholic Relief Act grants political emancipation to RCs.
     Peel's Metropolitan Police Act founds a professional police force in London.
     Lord William Bentinck, Governor General of India, prescribes as illegal the practice of Sati (immolation of a widow on her husband's funeral pyre).
     The first University boat race. Oxford beats Cambridge.

1830   Captain Swing agrarian riots against commons enclosures and threshing machines spread through southern England.

1831   Michael Faraday discovers Electro-magnetic induction leading to the invention of the electric transformer and generator.

1832   The Great Reform Act is passed. Rotten and pocket boroughs are abolished and replaced by constituencies in industrial towns; the franchise is extended to the urban upper middle class.
     The first of several cholera outbreaks kills many in London.
     Jeremy Bentham, the founder of Utilitarian philosophy, dies.

1832   cont. Sir Walter Scott, prolific Scottish writer and author of 'The Waverley Novels', dies of typhus.

1833   John Henry Newman and John Keble initiate the Anglo-Catholic Oxford Movement.

1834   Slavery is abolished throughout the British Empire.
        The Tolpuddle Martyrs are sentenced to 7 years transportation for taking an oath of secrecy as they try to establish a trade union.
        The Poor Law Amendment Act institutes the Union workhouse system and abolishes supplementary wages support for the poor (the Speenhamland System).
        Sir Robert Peel issues the Tamworth Manifesto, setting out the principles which will guide the future Conservative Party.
        Fire destroys the Houses of Parliament.

1836   The Tythe Commutation Act abolishes the ancient parish levy paid to church ministers.

11. The Imperial Era 1837 – 1901

1837   Queen Victoria ascends to the throne.
John Constable, the pre-eminent British landscape painter, dies.

1837-9 Charles Dickens serialises Oliver Twist, his earliest attempt to portray the social evils of nineteenth century Britain.

1838   Thomas Babington Macauley, historian, Whig politician and educationalist finishes his Lays of Ancient Rome.

1839   The first Chartist petition seeking radical const-itutional reforms is delivered to parliament.
24 are killed in a riot of Chartist sympathisers at Newport, Monmouthshire.
The Rebecca Riots about rural poverty break out in West Wales.
The first Grand National horse race and the first Henley Regatta take place.

1840   Rowland Hill introduces the pre-paid Penny Post paid for by the Penny Black, the world's first postage stamp.
The first steam-driven paddle steamer services are introduced - to Alexandria (P&O) - to Boston (Cunard).
The rebuilding of the Houses of Parliament (destroyed by fire 1834) begins, planned by Sir Charles Barry (completed 1860).
The Canadian provinces are unified under a single legislature.

1841   The Retreat from Kabul – 4,000 British troops and 12,000 others are lost. Start of the second Afghan War.
New Zealand becomes a colony.

!841   cont. Dr David Livingstone starts his missionary work in Central Africa.

James Ross explores Antarctica.

The first edition of Punch magazine is published.

1842   The treaty of Nanking ends the First Opium War with China. Hong Kong becomes a British colony.

The First peacetime Income Tax is introduced - seven pence in the pound.

The Mines Act forbids underground employment of women and children under ten.

1843   I. K. Brunel, Britain's engineering genius, launches the Great Britain, the first iron built, screw-driven passenger liner.

The Economist magazine begins publication.

1844   The Factory Act limits working hours – women 12 hours, children (8-13) six hours per day.

The first Cooperative shop opens in Rochdale.

1845   The Potato Famine starts in Ireland. The Great Irish migration to the USA begins.

The last sighting of Sir John Franklin's expedition to find the North West Passage via the Arctic to the Pacific.

1846   The Corn Laws are repealed by Peel's government in an attempt to ease hardship in Ireland and alleviate working class complaints about the price of bread.

Tory protectionist rebels led by Benjamin Disraeli split the party and eventually form the Conservative Party. The Peelite rump eventually merges with Free Trade Whigs to become the Liberal Party.

Using male pseudonyms, the Bronte sisters Charlotte, Emily and Ann (later to achieve fame for novels published under their own names) publish a collection of poems.

1847   Greenwich Mean Time is used as standardised time (Railway Time) throughout Great Britain, aided by the General Post Office telegraph service.

1848   The third Chartist Petition is presented to parliament.
        A year of revolutions in Europe – many refugees come to London.
        A group of young artists led by John E. Millais and Dante Gabriel Rossetti form the Pre-Raphaelite Brotherhood.
        Robert Fortune, a Scottish botanist, brings tea plants from China which enabled tea plantations to be established in India.
        The Public Health Act sets up the Board of Health.

1850   William Wordsworth, romantic poet and poet laureate, dies.

1851   The Great Exhibition promoted by Albert, the Prince Consort, opens in the Crystal Palace at Hyde Park.
        J. M. W. Turner, 'the supreme painter of light' (The Fighting Temeraire etc.) dies.

1852   The Duke of Wellington dies, celebrated by a State Funeral.

1853   William Gladstone's first Free Trade budget.

1854   Florence Nightingale and female nurses tend the sick and wounded of the Crimean War.
        Robert Fitzroy starts the Meteorological Office (now the Met Office) as a service to mariners.

1856   The Victoria Cross medal is instituted.

1857   The Indian Mutiny (or the First Indian War for Independence) starts in Meerut.

1858   Joseph Bazalgette plans a grand renewal of London's sewerage system after London experiences 'the Great Stink'.
        A transatlantic telegraph cable link to America is completed.
        The Irish Republican Brotherhood, a secret society aiming to establish an Irish republic, is founded in Dublin.

1859   Charles Darwin publishes The Origin of Species by Natural Selection, the foundation stone of evolutionary biology.
        The National Portrait Gallery opens.

1860   An Anglo-French force burns the Summer Palace in Peking (Beijing).
        The New Houses of Parliament are completed.
        The Royal Navy West Africa Squadron stands down having helped put an end to the international trans-Atlantic slave trade.
        The first British Open Golf championship is held at Prestwich.

1861   Albert the Prince Consort dies. Queen Victoria enters a period of withdrawal from national affairs.
        The Royal Horticultural Society (formerly The London Horticultural Society since 1804) which promotes gardening and botanical research and development is chartered.

1863   London's first underground 'tube' service from Paddington to Farringdon, opens.
        The Football Association is formed.

1864   The first County Cricket Championship is held.
        John Clare, the peasant poet, dies in Northampton lunatic asylum.

1865   The governor is recalled and dismissed after the brutal suppression of rebellion in Jamaica.

1865   cont. Alice's Adventures in Wonderland by Lewis
Carroll is published.

1867   Transportation of convicts to the colonies is ended.
        A Fenian uprising by the Irish Republican Brother-
hood is quashed.
        Karl Marx publishes the first volume of the socialist
bible Das Kapital, researched and written in London and
published in Hamburg.
        Antiseptic measures to prevent infection are first
used by Joseph Lister, professor of surgery at Glasgow.
        The Marquess of Queensbury Rules for the regulation
of Boxing are introduced.

1868   The last public hangings are held at Newgate and
Maidstone prisons.
        The first Trades Union Congress is held at
Manchester.

1869   Girton, the first college for women is founded at
Cambridge, but it only became part of the university in 1948.

1870   The Married Women's Property Act recognises wives'
rights to own and control property.
        William E. Forster's Education Act provides for
compulsory education of all children aged 5 to 12.
        Thomas Barnardo opens the first Dr. Barnardo's
orphanage in London's East End.

1871   The Trade Union Act legalises unions.
        Public holidays are instituted with the first Bank
Holiday on August 7th.
        The Rugby Football Union is founded.

1872   The first secret ballot is held in Great Britain at a
Pontefract bi-election.
        The first FA cup final is won by Wanderers.

1872   cont. The First international football match (Scotland 0 England 0).

1873   Dr. David Livingstone, missionary and explorer dies at Lake Bangwelu, Central Africa.
John Stuart Mill, the political economist and liberal philosopher dies.

1874   The Cavendish Laboratory of Experimental Physics opens in Cambridge.

1875   Disraeli purchases a majority stake in the Suez Canal Company for Britain.
Captain Matthew Webb is the first to swim across the English Channel.
The London Medical School for Women is established.
Ellen Terry performs as Portia in Shakespeare's 'The Merchant of Venice' to great acclaim for her artistry and beauty.

1876   Queen Victoria is declared Empress of India.
Merchant Shipping Act measures include the Plimsoll line to prevent overloading of vessels.

1877   The first All England Croquet and Lawn Tennis Championship is held at Wimbledon.

1878   William Booth founds the Salvation Army, a Christian evangelical and charitable movement.

1879   Somerville and Lady Margaret Hall colleges for women are founded at Oxford.
Electric street lighting is introduced in London at the Embankment and Waterloo Bridge.

1880   Cecil Rhodes founds the De Beers diamond mining company in South Africa.

1880   cont. Mary Anne Evans, alias George Eliot, author of powerful novels such as Middlemarch, dies.

1881   Richard D'Oyly Carte opens the Savoy Theatre for the production of Gilbert and Sullivan's light operas.
    Thomas Carlyle, Scottish historian, lecturer and essayist, dies.

1882   Britain assumes the unofficial position of de facto Protector of Egypt.
    The Phoenix Park murders; Fenians kill Lord Frederick Cavendish, Chief Secretary of Ireland, and the Permanent under Secretary Thomas Henry Burke.
    Australia defeats England in a Test Match at the Oval and 'The Ashes' are created.

1883   Karl Marx, communist philosopher dies and is buried at Highgate cemetery.

1884   The Third Parliamentary Reform Act extends male suffrage - farm workers get the vote.
    Greenwich chosen as the world's Prime Meridian (0 degree Longitude).
    The Fabian Society is created to propagate socialist ideas.
    James Murray begins work on the Oxford English Dictionary.
    Lord Shaftesbury founds The London Society for the Prevention of Cruelty to Children (renamed National Society for Prevention of Cruelty to Children in 1889).

1885   General Gordon is killed at Khartoum in the Sudan.
    The Criminal Law Amendment Act raises the age of sexual consent for girls to 16.

1886   The first Home Rule for Ireland bill is defeated.

1887   The Arts and Crafts Exhibition Society is formed to promote high quality and functional decorative art and crafts.

1888   Jack the Ripper brutally murders 6 women in London's East End.
        The Football League is formed with 12 participating clubs.

1889   The British South Africa Company is chartered to promote settlement in what was to become Southern Rhodesia (Zimbabwe).

1890   Millicent Fawcett becomes president of the National Union of Women's Suffrage Societies.

1892   Alfred Lord Tennyson, poet laureate during much of Victoria's reign, dies.
        The Theatre Royal, Covent Garden is renamed the Royal Opera House.

1893   The Independent Labour Party is founded by Keir Hardie.

1894   William E. Gladstone retires after a career in politics lasting more than 60 years.
        Dame Edith Brown founds The Christian Medical College for women in the Punjab, India.
        The Memoirs of Sherlock Holmes by Conan Doyle and the Jungle Book by Rudyard Kipling are published.

1895   Oscar Wilde, playwright and wit is sent to gaol for committing an act of gross indecency.
        The National Trust is founded by Octavia Hill.
        The London School of Economics and Political Science is founded.
        The Northern Union of Rugby Football clubs is formed (changed its name to the Rugby Football League in 1922).

1896   The Daily Mail newspaper is published for the first time.
        Death of William Morris, the influential Arts and Crafts designer, poet and socialist.
        The British East Africa Company starts construction of the Uganda Railway from Mombasa which opens up East Africa for colonial development.

1897   Queen Victoria's Diamond Jubilee is celebrated.
        The Tate Gallery of British Art opens.
        Charles Rennie Mackintosh, influential architect and designer, begins work on his eponymous Glasgow School building.

1898   The last cavalry charge by the British army takes place at the Battle of Omdurman. Khartoum is retaken and the Sudan is to be ruled by an Anglo-Egyptian government.

1899   The 2nd Boer War begins in South Africa.
        London's first motor bus service begins.
        Sir Edward Elgar's Enigma Variations is performed in London.

1900   Britain takes part in the suppression of the Boxer rising in Peking (Beijing).

1901   Queen Victoria dies.

12. Before the Storm 1901 -1913

1901   cont. The six Australian colonies form the Common-
wealth of Australia.
Guglielmo Marconi sends a wireless message from
Cornwall to Newfoundland.
The British Academy for study of the Humanities and
Natural Science is founded.

1902   Cecil Rhodes, financier and imperialist in Africa, dies
leaving money to fund Rhodes Scholarships at Oxford
University.
Sir Ronald Ross becomes the first British Nobel prize
winner (Medicine) for discovering that mosquitoes transmit
malaria.

1903   Mrs Emmeline Pankhurst forms the Women's Social
and Political Union (later known as the Suffragette
movement).
The Anglo-French Entente Cordiale is agreed during
Edward VII's visit to Paris.

1904   The first Rolls Royce motor car is produced.

1905   The Aliens Act safeguards the right of political asylum
to immigrants.
Work starts on a pioneer garden city at Letchworth
according to the precepts of Ebenezer Howard.

1906   The Parliamentary Labour Party is founded.
Joseph John Thompson wins the Nobel Prize (Physics)
for work on the electron in atomic physics.

1907   Sinn Fein is created to seek self-government in
Ireland.

1907   cont. The Dominion of New Zealand is created.
        General Baden-Powell starts the Scouting movement
with a camp at Brownsea Island.
        The world's first motor racing track opens at
Brooklands, Surrey.

1908   The Old Age Pension Act marks the beginning of
Britain's social welfare system - people aged over 70 receive 5
shillings per week.
        Ernest Rutherford wins the Nobel Prize (Chemistry)
for researches in nuclear chemistry.
        The first purpose built cinema in Britain opens at
Colne Lancashire.
        The Wind in the Willows by Kenneth Grahame is
published.

1909   Lloyd George's 'People's Budget' leads to parliamentary conflict about the powers of the House of Lords.
        The Union of South Africa is proclaimed a dominion.
        MI5 counter espionage organisation is formed.
        The Victoria and Albert Museum opens.
        The Girl Guides movement is formed.

1911   Lloyd George introduces a National Insurance
scheme.
        The Parliament Act restricting the powers of the
House of Lords is passed.
        The Official Secrets Act is passed.

1912   The Ulster Covenant resisting Home Rule for Ireland is
signed by hundreds of thousands of Unionists.
        The Titanic ocean liner collides with an iceberg and
sinks.
        Captain Robert F. Scott's expedition to the South Pole
ends in tragedy.

1913   The Ulster Volunteer Force is raised to oppose Irish Home Rule 'by force if necessary'.

The Irish Volunteers is founded under the auspices of the Irish Republican Brotherhood (IRB) in response to the UVF.

Emily Davidson, a suffragette, throws herself under the king's horse and dies at the Epsom Derby.

The New Statesman magazine is first published under the auspices of the Fabian Society.

13. Two World Wars 1914 – 1945

1914   The Great War (WWI) starts. A Serbian kills the crown prince of Austro-Hungary which declares war on Serbia, whose ally Russia, in alliance with France, declare war on Austria-Hungary and its ally Germany. Germany invades Belgium to get at France. Great Britain declares war on Germany to honour its commitment to Belgium.

1915   German Zeppelin airships bomb English towns and cities including London.
    The British Expeditionary force to France and Flanders is decimated in the opening months of the war. Imperial forces arrive to assist.
    Lord Kitchener raises a volunteer army.
    Gallipoli landings with British, Australian and New Zealand troops suffering severe losses as they try to cut off Turkey from its European allies.
    Chlorine gas is used against British troops at the 2nd battle of Ypres.
    Nurse Edith Cavell is shot as a spy by the Germans.
    Rupert Brooke, author of War Sonnets which includes The Soldier poem, dies en route to the Dardanelles in Greece.
    William L. Bragg, 25, becomes the youngest Nobel Prize winner for work on X-ray crystallography with his father Sir William H. Bragg.

1916   The Battle of the Somme - 20,000 British troops, many of Kitchener's new army, are killed on the first day.
    The Military Service Act introduces conscription of civilian men into the armed services.
    Naval battle at Jutland is inconclusive but leaves the Royal Navy in control of the North Sea.
    Lloyd George becomes prime minister.
    The Easter Rising in Dublin organised by the Irish Volunteers and the IRB is put down, but execution of the

1916   cont. leaders and harsh actions by the British authorities fuel nationalist resentment in Ireland.

Sykes-Picot agreement delineates spheres of Anglo-French control and influence in the post-war Middle East.

Sir Ernest Shackleton completes his epic story of endurance with the rescue of all his Antarctic expedition comrades left stranded on a remote island.

1917   T. E. Lawrence directs the Arab insurgency at the capture of Aqaba and continues to harry the Turks in Arabia and Palestine.

The Balfour Declaration promises a Jewish homeland in Palestine.

The German name of the Royal family is changed to Windsor.

The Irish Republican Army (IRA) is formed to fight for an independent Ireland.

Tanks are used ineffectively at the battle of Passchendaele due to thick mud.

1918   The German Spring Offensive breaks through British lines but is contained.

The Battle of Amiens, German lines on the Western Front are destroyed by Imperial forces. Allied forces begin the 100 Days Offensive which ends with the Armistice which terminates the Great War.

The Royal Air Force is founded.

Wilfred Owen, celebrated war poet, is killed one week before the armistice.

Women over 30 with property vote for the first time in the General Election.

Sinn Fein candidates win a majority in Ireland but don't take their seats in Westminster.

1919   The Treaty of Versailles ends the Great War and inflicts punitive reparations on Germany.

1919   cont. British troops commanded by General Reginald Dyer massacre 379 Indians at Jallianwala Bagh, Amritsar.

Nancy, Lady Astor becomes the first woman Member of Parliament to take her seat.

My Man Jeeves is published by P. G. Wodehouse.

John Alcock and Arthur Brown fly an aeroplane non-stop across the Atlantic.

1920   The Government of Ireland Act proposes divided Home Rule for South of Ireland (Dublin) and Ulster (Belfast).

A Royal Irish Constabulary unit fires on a football crowd at Croke Park in Dublin killing twelve civilians.

The Communist Party of Great Britain is founded.

1921   The Red Poppy is worn for first time at the Remembrance Day ceremony in memory of those who fell in the Great War.

The separate Parliament of Northern Ireland meets in Belfast.

Marie Stopes opens the first Mothers' Clinic advocating birth control in London.

1922   A provisional government headed by Michael Collins takes office in Dublin and fights a brief civil war with the IRA. Collins is killed and the Irish Free State is established as a dominion under the crown.

'Music Hall Queen' Marie Lloyd is taken ill on stage and dies aged 52.

The British Broadcasting Company (BBC), under the management of John (later Lord) Reith, begins radio transmissions from Marconi House in The Strand.

The British Protectorate of Egypt ends.

Howard Carter discovers the tomb of Tutankhamun in Egypt.

1923   The first FA cup final is held at Wembley stadium, Bolton Wanderers 2 West Ham United 1.

1924   Joseph Conrad, Polish-born English language novelist, dies.

The British Empire Exhibition opens at Wembley.

1925   Cyprus, with a mixed Greek-Turkish population, becomes a crown colony.

George Bernard Shaw, Anglo-Irish writer and critic, receives the Nobel Prize in Literature.

1926   A General Strike is called and ends after eight days.

A. A. Milne creates the first collection of Winnie-the-Pooh stories.

The First British greyhound track opens at Belle Vue, Manchester.

The Council for The Preservation of Rural England is founded.

1928   The Equal Franchise Act gives votes to all women aged over 21.

Alexander Fleming discovers penicillin at St Mary's hospital, Paddington.

The Flying Scotsman steam engine starts operating on the London-Edinburgh railway line.

Thomas Hardy, poet and writer of novels about life in semi-mythical Wessex, dies.

1929   The Wall Street crash signals the beginning of a world financial slump.

Margaret Bondfield, Minister of Labour in the new Labour government, become the first woman member of the cabinet and Privy Councillor.

The first public telephone boxes come into service.

1930   Mahatma Gandhi starts a civil disobedience campaign in India.

John Maynard Keynes publishes A Treatise on Money.
The Youth Hostels Association is established.

1931   The Ministry of Transport issues the first Highway Code.
        Britain leaves the Gold Standard as financial problems deepen.
        Lilian Baylis and Ninette de Valois start the Vic-Wells Ballet Company, later to become Sadlers Wells.

1932   Import Duties Act introduces tariffs – end of the Free Trade era. Steps are taken to establish Imperial preference in trade.
        Sir Oswald Mosley founds the British Union of Fascists.
        George V makes the first royal Christmas broadcast.
        Ernest Walton and John Cockcroft, both to be Nobel Prize winners, perform a controlled split of an atomic nucleus at the Cavendish laboratory, Cambridge.
        The Shakespeare Memorial Theatre, Stratford on Avon, opens.
        Sir Thomas Beecham founds the London Philharmonic Orchestra.
        Alexander Korda founds London Film Productions at Denham studios.
        Brave New World, a novel by Aldous Huxley, is published.

1933   Adolph Hitler becomes Chancellor of Germany;
        Winston Churchill makes his first speech about the dangers of German rearmament.
        The MCC's 'bodyline tour' of Australia causes discord in the cricket world.
        The National Playing Fields Association is created.

1934   The Glyndbourne opera festival is founded.

1935   The Greenbelt is established around London.
        Penguin Books Ltd begins to print paperback books.

1936   Edward VIII becomes king but abdicates so that he can marry Wallis Simpson, an American divorcee.

The Jarrow Marchers protest about high unemployment.

The first flight of the Supermarine Spitfire fighter plane designed by R. J. Mitchell.

The BBC begins transmitting a TV service from Alexandra Palace.

Billy Butlin opens his first holiday camp at Skegness.

1937   The Irish Free State is re-named Eire and becomes an independent state within the Commonwealth but owes no allegiance to the crown.

Frank Whittle demonstrates his jet propulsion engine.

1938   Neville Chamberlain tries to appease Adolph Hitler by agreeing to the secession of Sudetenland from Czechoslovakia. German troops enter Sudetenland.

Bletchley Park is bought privately by the head of MI6 as a potential home for enemy communications analysis in the event of war breaking out.

1939   Germany invades Poland and ignores British demands to withdraw. World War II begins.

Anglo-Saxon burial ship treasure is excavated at Sutton Hoo.

1940   Winston Churchill becomes Prime Minister. "We shall never surrender" the first of his wartime speeches.

Most of the British Expeditionary Force is rescued from Dunkirk as France falls.

The Channel Islands are occupied by German troops.

The Battle of Britain. The RAF prevents the Luftwaffe establishing air superiority in preparation for a military invasion.

The Blitz (heavy and destructive air raids on London and other cities) commences.

1940   cont. Food rationing (bacon, butter, sugar) is introduced.

1941   Germany attacks the Soviet Union. Britain begins to send aid via Arctic Convoys to Russia.
    HMS Hood is sunk in the Atlantic sea battle which ends with the sinking of the German battleship Bismarck.
    Japan invades Hong Kong and Malaya on the same day as the Pearl Harbour attack.
    United States enters war against the Axis (Germany, Italy and Japan) powers.

1942   Singapore falls to Japanese troops.
    The Avro Lancaster enters service with RAF Bomber Command.
    Malta is awarded the George Cross for withstanding Axis air raids over four months.
    The Eighth Army under General Montgomery defeats Rommel's Afrika Korps at El Alamein.
    The Beveridge Report advocates state-assisted social care 'from cradle to grave'.

1943   RAF Dambusters 617 Squadron attacks the Ruhr dams with Barnes Wallis's 'bouncing bombs'.
    Viscount Samuel describes Nazi persecution of Jews as a 'Holocaust' in House of Lords.

1944   D Day. Allied forces commanded by US General Eisenhower land on the Normandy beaches.
    V-1 (flying bomb or doodlebug) and V-2 rockets commence bombardment of London.
    The bridge over the lower Rhine at Arnhem is attacked by British airborne forces with severe losses.
    General Bill Slim's 'forgotten' 14th Army defeats Japanese force trying to invade India at Imphal and begins to retake Burma.

1944   cont. R. A. Butler's Education Act introduces free secondary education with 11 plus exam to determine eligibility for grammar, technical or 'modern' secondary schools.

1945   Massive air raids by RAF Bomber Command and the USAAF destroy the German city of Dresden.

Field Marshall Montgomery accepts German un-conditional surrender.

VE day (Victory in Europe) celebrations.

British troops enter the Belsen concentration camp and discover horrific conditions.

VJ day. Japan surrenders after USA drops two nuclear bombs on Japanese cities.

End of World War II

14. Fresh Start 1949 -1951

1945   cont. Labour led By Clement Attlee wins the General Election with a policy of social improvement and the national-isation of major industries and commercial enterprises.
Animal Farm by George Orwell is published.
Brief Encounter, a romantic film directed by David Lean, is released.

1946   The Bank of England is nationalised.
Churchill makes his 'Iron Curtain' speech at Fulton, Missouri, warning of the Soviet Union threat in Europe.
Jewish terrorists blow up the King David Hotel, the British HQ in Jerusalem.
London Airport opens at Heath Row.
The Arts Council of Great Britain is inaugurated.

1947   Severe winter followed by flooding then a hot, dry summer exacerbates fuel and food shortages.
Coal is the first major industry to be nationalised.
Exchange controls restrict movement of capital out of the country followed by further austerity measures.
India's independence is recognised and the country is partitioned into two sovereign states – Republic of India and Islamic Pakistan. Mass sectarian slaughters as people attempt to flee across the new borders.
Princess Elizabeth marries Philip, Duke of Edinburgh.
The first Edinburgh Festival of the Arts opens.

1948   Aneurin Bevan oversees the creation of the National Health Service.
Britain withdraws from its mandate in Palestine. An Arab-Jewish war ensues and ends with the creation of the State of Israel.

1948   cont. Britain takes part in the Berlin Airlift in response to a Soviet blockade of the Western powers' zones of control in the city.

The National Party gains power in South Africa and begins the Apartheid racial segregation policy.

The British Nationality Act grants British citizenship to all Commonwealth citizens.

The Empire Windrush arrives at Tilbury with the first batch of immigrants from the West Indies.

The XII Olympiad is held at Wembley.

The Landrover utility vehicle goes on sale.

T.S. Eliot, Anglo-American poet and playwright, wins the Nobel Prize in Literature.

The Red Shoes, a film produced and directed by Powell and Pressburger, is released.

1949   Britain is a founder-member of the North Atlantic Treaty Organisation (NATO) formed to resist Soviet aggression.

The Pound sterling is devalued – from $4.03 to $2.80.

Eire becomes the Republic of Ireland and leaves the Commonwealth of Nations, composed of former imperial territories, which drops the word British from its title.

The maiden flight of the De Havilland Comet, the world's first jet airliner.

British military operations begin against communist guerrillas in Malaya.

1984, a novel by George Orwell, is published.

BBC Radio begins broadcasts of the Goon Show, a surreal British comedy series.

The film Passport to Pimlico, one of a classic run of Ealing Comedies, is released.

Thomas the Tank Engine by the Rev. W. Awdry is published.

1950   British troops are part of the UN force sent to South Korea to repel an invasion by North Korea.

1950   cont. The House of Commons chamber re-opens following restoration after bomb damage.

J Sainsbury opens the first British purpose-built supermarket in Croydon.

The Stone of Scone is taken from the Coronation Chair in Westminster Abbey by Scots nationalists.

The Third Man, a classic mystery/thriller film directed by Carol Reed, screen-play by Graham Greene, is released.

Bertrand Russell wins the Nobel Prize in Literature.

1951   The Festival of Britain begins and the Royal Festival Hall is opened.

Guy Burgess and Donald MacLean, members of the Cambridge spy ring, defect to the Soviet Union.

Winston Churchill returns as prime minister after Conservatives win the General Election.

The first volume of Nicholas Pevsner's Buildings of England is published.

The first episode of The Archers, the world's longest-running soap opera, is broadcast on BBC radio.

15. Adjustment and Retrenchment 1952 – 1979

1952   Princess Elizabeth, whilst touring Kenya, becomes Queen Elizabeth II on the death of her father George VI.

Britain tests its first nuclear bomb.

The Great London Smog kills over 2000.

A State of Emergency is declared in Kenya following Mau Mau activities.

The Mousetrap by best-selling mystery writer Agatha Christie begins a record-breaking run in the West End.

1953   Nobel Prize winners Francis Crick and James Watson present a model demonstrating the double helix structure of DNA.

Loss of life as the East Coast suffers a severe tidal surge.

The coronation of Queen Elizabeth II takes place.

Casino Royale, the first James Bond novel by Ian Fleming is published.

1954   Food rationing ends.

Roger Bannister runs a mile in 3 minutes 59.4 secs, breaking the 4 minute barrier.

Lord of the Flies by William Golding and Fellowship of the Ring by J.R.R. Tolkien are published.

Dylan Thomas, Welsh poet, dies 11 weeks after BBC Radio broadcasts Under Milk Wood.

1955   Ruth Ellis is the last woman to be executed in Britain.

ITV begins a TV service with commercial advertising.

The Duke of Edinburgh Award Scheme is inaugurated.

Sir Laurence Olivier's film production of Richard III is released.

1956   Calder Hall, the world's first nuclear power station, opens.

1956   cont. The first anti–nuclear Aldermaston march takes place.

Sadlers Wells becomes the Royal Ballet Company.

The Clean Air Act introduces smoke control areas for some cities.

Premium Bonds are introduced.

The Suez Canal is nationalised by Egypt. Anglo-French military attempt to seize the canal fails.

1957   Harold Macmillan becomes Prime Minister after Sir Anthony Eden resigns.

The Wolfenden Report recommends homosexual acts between consenting adults should no longer be an offence.

Ghana, formerly the Gold Coast, is the first black African colony to become independent. The Malay Federation also becomes independent.

1958   The Campaign for Nuclear Disarmament (CND) led by Bertrand Russell and Canon John Collins is launched.

Race riots break out in Notting Hill, London.

Four women are among the first life peers to sit in the House of Lords.

Ralph Vaughan Williams dies four months after the premier of his 9th Symphony.

Eight Manchester United players are killed when their plane crashes at Munich airport.

1959   Singapore and Cyprus become independent.

Southern part of the M1, Britain's first inter-urban motorway, opens.

The Morris Mini car designed by Alec Issigonis goes on sale.

1960   MacMillan delivers his 'Wind of Change' speech in Cape Town about the decolonisation of Africa.

Coronation Street, an iconic and long-running soap opera begins on ITV.

1960   cont. The Commonwealth War Graves Commission is renamed with a mandate to care for war graves/memorials of all Imperial troops killed in past conflicts.

Nigeria becomes independent.

The end of National Service conscription into the armed services.

The Caretaker by Harold Pinter is first performed at the Arts Theatre, London.

The premiere of Oliver!, a musical based on Oliver Twist by Lionel Bart, takes place at the New Theatre, London.

Beyond the Fringe, a seminal satirical revue starring Peter Cook, Dudley Moore, Alan Bennet and Jonathan Miller, opens at the Edinburgh Festival.

Lady Chatterley's Lover trial; Penguin Books is cleared of publishing an obscene book.

1961   South Africa leaves the Commonwealth after concerted criticism of apartheid.

Peter Hall forms the Royal Shakespeare Company.

Britain gives up the Protectorate of Kuwait (since 1899).

The first Comedy Playhouse TV series is broadcast, a launch pad for many BBC sit-coms.

The Prime of Miss Jean Brodie, a novel by Muriel Spark, is published.

The University of Sussex opens - first of a new tranche of regional universities.

1962   The Commonwealth Immigration Act withdraws the principle of free entry to Britain for all Commonwealth citizens. Uganda becomes independent.

Benjamin Britten's War Requiem with Wilfred Owen poems is performed in the new Coventry cathedral.

Margot Fonteyn's career at the Royal Ballet is reignited by her partnership with Rudolph Nureyev.

The last Gentlemen v Players cricket match takes place at Lords (held since 1806).

1963   The Beeching Report recommends a drastic reduction of the British Rail network.

The Profumo Scandal shakes the government.

Kim Philby is named as 'the third man' in the Cambridge spy ring.

The Beatles debut album Please Please Me is released.

John Le Carre publishes The Spy Who Came in From the Cold.

The Gillette Cup is inaugurated - the first one day knockout cricket event.

The Great Train Robbers steal £2.5million from a Royal Mail express train.

Joan Plowright's Theatre Workshop performs Oh What a Lovely War.

The first performance by the National Theatre Company takes place at the Old Vic.

1964   The Sun newspaper starts publication.

Kenya becomes independent.

Peter A. Allen and Gwynne O. Evans are the last persons to be executed by hanging in the UK.

1965   The State funeral of Sir Winston Churchill takes place at St Paul's Cathedral.

The death penalty for murder is abolished.

The Labour Government publishes circular 10/65 which promotes comprehensive education.

Dame Elizabeth Lane becomes the first woman judge.

The Race Relations Act forbids public racial discrimination.

Ian Smith, prime minister of Southern Rhodesia, declares unilateral independence.

1965   Sir Stanley Matthews retires and is the first footballer to be knighted.

1965   cont.   The death of Richard Dimbleby, eminent radio/TV broadcaster.

1966   Sectarian divisions in Northern Ireland - Rev. Ian Paisley refounds the Ulster Volunteer Force.
        Sir Alf Ramsey steers England to victory in the football World Cup at Wembley.
        The Aberfan Disaster. Coal spoil tip engulfs a school killing 116 children, 28 adults in South Wales.
        The government imposes a six month Prices and Incomes freeze.
        The first British Ombudsman is appointed.
        Ian Brady and Myra Hindley are convicted for the Moors Murders.
        Barbados and other territories continue the programme of colonial independence.
        Mary Quant, designer of the miniskirt and youth fashions is awarded the OBE.

1967   The Pound is devalued from $2.80 to $2.40.
        De Gaulle vetoes British application to join the EEC (Common Market) for a second time.
        The National Front neo-fascist party is formed.
        The Abortion Act, introduced by Liberal MP David Steel, legalises abortion in the UK.
        It is announced that British forces are to withdraw from East of Suez within eight years. Troops quit Aden.
        Gibraltar referendum: overwhelming result in favour of retaining British sovereignty.
        The breathalyser apparatus to test motor drivers for alcohol consumption is introduced.
        Colour TV service is introduced on BBC2.
        Sir Francis Chichester completes solo world circumnavigation in Gypsy Moth II.

1968   the Commonwealth Immigration Act limits intake of Kenyan Asians by a voucher system.

1968   cont. Enoch Powell makes 'Rivers of Blood' speech about Commonwealth immigration.

The Metrication Board is set up to oversee metrification of measurements.

Prices and Incomes Act brings back wages control.

The Royal Navy dockyard at Singapore is closed.

Theatrical censorship by the Lord Chamberlain is ended.

Sectarian 'Troubles' begin in Northern Ireland.

1969   Barbara Castle fails to get 'In place of Strife', white paper to improve industrial relations, approved by cabinet colleagues.

The Divorce Reform Act makes divorce easier.

The Open University is established (TV courses begin in 1971).

The Anglo-French built Concorde supersonic aircraft makes its maiden flight.

Civilisation, a cultural landmark TV documentary by Kenneth Clark, is broadcast on BBC 2.

Monty Python's Flying Circus, surreal TV comedy is broadcast on BBC 2.

Sir Noel Coward, playwright, composer and actor, is knighted.

Drugs-related death of Brian Jones, founder/member of the Rolling Stones R & B group.

1970   The Legal Age for voting is reduced to eighteen.

The IRA splits and the militant wing forms the Provisional IRA.

The Female Eunuch, feminist treatise by Germaine Greer is published.

Michael Eavis inaugurates the first Glastonbury Festival (then called the Pilton Festival).

Ian Macleod, Chancellor of the Exchequer in a new Conservative government, dies.

1971   Decimal coinage replaces shillings and pence.
British forces pull out of Malta.
Foundation of Campaign for Real Ale (CAMRA) to support real ale and the traditional British pub.
Stairway to Heaven, influential rock anthem, composed by Robert Plant and Jimmy Page is released by rock group Led Zeppelin.

1972   'Bloody Sunday' in Londonderry. British troops kill 13 demonstrators.
Direct rule from Westminster imposed on Northern Ireland (lifted briefly and re-introduced in 1974).
40,000 Asians expelled from Uganda. Refugees begin to arrive in Britain.
Sir John Betjeman, poet and heritage campaigner, becomes Poet Laureate.
Jesus Christ Superstar composed by Tim Rice, Andrew Lloyd Webber becomes first of a new generation of British West End musical hits.
David Bowie, popular music superstar, starts his Ziggy Stardust era.

1973   Britain, Ireland and Denmark join the original six in the European Economic Community (The 'Common Market').
Value Added Tax is introduced.
The Conservative government imposes 3 day working week in response to power difficulties caused by miners' union overtime ban.
Peter Hall succeeds Lord Olivier as director of the National Theatre.

1974   'Who Governs Britain?' Two general elections in one year return Harold Wilson's Labour Party to power with a 'Social Contract' policy agreed with trade union leaders.
The Prevention of Terrorism Act responds to fatal IRA bombings on mainland Britain.

1974   cont. Lord Lucan disappears following the murder of his children's nanny.

1975   Margaret Thatcher becomes the leader of the Conservative party.
        British membership of the EEC is approved by a referendum vote.
        North Sea oil begins to be piped ashore to Grangemouth in Scotland.
        Sex Discrimination Act enforces equal opportunity for women job applicants.
        Women's Equal Pay Act comes into force.

1976   Surprise resignation of Harold Wilson. Succeeded as prime minister by James Callaghan.
        Heavy cuts in government expenditure in return for a loan from the International Monetary Fund (IMF) after a run on the pound.
        Race Relations Act reinforces anti-discrimination law.
        Direct grant payments to certain grammar schools are phased out.

1977   Lib-Lab Pact – Liberals agree to prop up the Labour government on a range of issues.
        Sex Pistols achieve height of Punk Rock fame/infamy with their version of 'God Save the Queen'.
        Red Rum wins the Grand National for the third time.
        Islamic Cultural Centre mosque opens at Regents Park London.

1978   Dutch Elm disease now afflicts over 80% of the tree species in Britain.
        Louise Joy Brown, world's first IVF 'test tube baby', is born at Oldham.
        Naomi James is the first woman to sail single-handed around the world.

16. Reformation and Change 1979 - 1997

1979   'The Winter of Discontent'. Widespread industrial action by public service workers opposed to government pay restraint policy.

A small majority vote in favour of devolution in a Scottish referendum. A large majority oppose devolution in a Welsh referendum.

Margaret Thatcher becomes the UK's first woman prime minister.

Airy Neave MP, Conservative spokesman for Northern Ireland, is killed by an IRA car bomb in the House of Commons car park.

Earl Mountbatten and family members are blown up by an IRA bomb; 18 soldiers killed by IRA at Warren Point, South Armagh.

First British elections for the European Parliament.

Exchange controls are removed and the Prices Commission is abolished – the first Thatcherite economic moves.

David Attenborough presents Life on Earth, first of his Life series of TV programmes.

The Times resumes publication after year long closure caused by a labour dispute about manning levels and new technology.

Margot Fonteyn's unofficial retirement is marked by Covent Garden gala to mark her 60th birthday.

1980   Southern Rhodesia becomes the independent republic of Zimbabwe.

SAS rescues hostages held by dissidents in the Iranian embassy. First TV viewing of Special Forces in action.

The First Thatcherite move to regulate trade union activities - Employment Act limits secondary picketing and closed shop activities.

Housing Act allows tenants to buy council houses.

Unemployment rises to over 2 million (9% of the workforce).

1980   cont. Ex-Beatles performer/songwriter John Lennon is shot dead in New York.

1981   Women set up a peace camp at Greenham Common, American base for cruise missiles.

Gang of Four ex Labour MPs form the Social Democratic party.

Bobby Sands, a Sinn Fein MP on hunger strike, dies in the Maze prison.

Charles, Prince of Wales, marries Lady Diana Spencer.

Pound coins replace notes.

1982   Argentina invades the Falkland Islands – retaken by a British task force two and half months later.

The Marie Rose, sunk in 1545, is recovered from the seabed near Portsmouth.

The Thames Flood Barrier is completed.

1983   Isle of Dogs becomes an Enterprise Zone to encourage redevelopment in East London.

English Heritage is re-formed under Lord Montagu to care for the National Heritage Collection and other heritage matters.

Lester Piggott rides his ninth and final Epsom Derby winner, Crepello.

1984   Miners' Strike to protest against pit closures is called.

Margaret Thatcher announces she could do business with Mikhail Gorbachev of the Soviet Union.

British Telecom is the first of Thatcher government's major privatisations.

Mrs Thatcher survives an IRA bomb blast which wrecks the Grand Hotel, Brighton during the Conservative Party Conference.

1984   cont. WPC Yvonne Fletcher is shot dead by a gunman from within the Libyan embassy.

The AIDS disease is found to be affecting some of the British population.

1985   The Miners' Strike ends.

Live Aid concert at Wembley stadium raises funds for African famine relief.

Riot kills 38 at Liverpool v Juventus football match in the Heysel stadium, Brussels. FIFA bans English clubs competng abroad.

Philip Larkin, poet and librarian, dies.

1986   Rupert Murdoch moves News International printing operation to Wapping followed by a year-long dispute with the print unions. End of Fleet Street as the newspaper centre.

Phantom of the Opera by Andrew Lloyd Webber confirms Cameron Mackintosh as Britain's most successful theatrical producer.

Nissan is the first Japanese company to operate a British car plant - in Sunderland.

Unemployment reaches three and quarter million.

The 'Big Bang'. Financial markets are deregulated and electronic trading begins on the London Stock Exchange.

1987   IRA bomb at Enniskillen Remembrance Day parade kills 11.

The Docklands Light Railway, the first driverless, computerised train service in the UK, starts operating.

1988   New pub licencing laws allow all day opening in England and Wales.

Mrs Thatcher delivers the Bruges speech opposing further centralisation of European power.

The first series of Talking Heads by Alan Bennett is broadcast by BBC TV.

1989   Tim Berners-Lee, British inventor of the world-wide web, makes the first communication via the internet.

The Community Charge tax to pay for local government (known as the Poll Tax) is introduced in Scotland.

Britain is at variance with Commonwealth countries over sanctions against South Africa's apartheid policy.

95 Liverpool fans die at FA Cup semi-final in Hillsborough stadium, Sheffield.

The Labour Party national Executive drops the clause 4 nationalisation policy from the party's constitution.

TV coverage of House of Commons proceedings begins.

Sky provides the first British satellite TV service.

1990   Violent demonstration in London against the Poll Tax.

Britain and wartime allies sign the Moscow Treaty of Final Settlement with Germany, following demolition of the Berlin wall and widespread uprisings in the Soviet bloc.

Mrs Thatcher resigns after failing to secure a decisive win in first stage of a Conservative party leadership election.

Nelson Mandela is released from prison in South Africa.

1991   The IRA launches a mortar bomb attack on Downing Street during a cabinet meeting. John Major and cabinet members are not injured.

British armed forces take part in the First Iraq War which liberates Kuwait.

The Soviet Union dissolves into separate states.

Death of Graham Greene, Catholic novelist and film script writer.

Alfred Wainwright, composer of iconic guides to the English Lakeland, dies.

1992   'Black Wednesday'- The pound sterling crashes out of the European Exchange Rate Mechanism designed to bring currencies into alignment in preparation for launch of the Euro currency.

Betty Boothroyd MP becomes first woman Speaker of the House of Commons.

The queen's 'Annus horribilis' –failure of marriages in the royal family and fire at Windsor Castle.

Elizabeth David, doyen of British food and cookery writers, dies.

The Church of England approves ordination of women priests.

The FA Premier League is formed by leading Anglo-Welsh football clubs.

1993   The UK becomes a member of the renamed European Union with ratification of the Treaty of Maastricht.

The Anti Federalist League is renamed the United Kingdom Independence Party (UKIP).

1994   The Channel Tunnel opens. First Eurostar London to Paris rail service.

Tony Blair becomes leader of the Labour Party following the death of John Smith.

Queen Elizabeth II makes a state visit to Russia.

The Sunday Trading Act allows most shops to open on Sundays.

1995   Queen Elizabeth II makes a state visit to post-apartheid South Africa and its new president Nelson Mandela.

Barings, Britain's oldest merchant bank, collapses after losses made by a rogue trader in Singapore.

Seamus Heaney, Northern Irish poet is awarded the Nobel Prize in Literature.

1996   Dolly the sheep is cloned at the Roslin Institute, Scotland.

The Stone of Scone is returned to Scotland.

Frankie Dettori wins seven out of seven races at Ascot.

Divorces of the Prince and Princess of Wales and the Duke and Duchess of York.

17. Fundamental Adjustments 1997 – 2015

1997   Tony Blair wins a crushing election victory and forms a New Labour government.

Diana Princess of Wales dies in a Paris car crash.

Hong Kong returns to Chinese rule. End of the British Empire.

Proposed devolution of government powers receives referendum majorities in Scotland and Wales.

Government allows the Bank of England to assume responsibility for UK monetary policy.

Harry Potter and the Philosopher's Stone is published, the first Harry Potter book by J. K. Rowling.

The British Library moves to a new home at Euston Road London.

The Royal yacht Britannia is decommissioned.

Laurie Lee, poet and novelist, dies.

1998   The Good Friday Agreement, an international and inter-party accord to resolve Northern Irish problems peaceably, is signed.

An explosion set off by the Real IRA kills 29 at Omagh, Northern Ireland.

South Crofty, the last tin mine in Cornwall closes.

Ted Hughes, poet, dies.

1999   The Euro currency is adopted in some European Union countries – the UK retains the £ sterling.

A limit of 93 hereditary peers is allowed to sit in the partly reformed House of Lords which now consists of mainly appointed members.

A new Assembly at Stormont restores self-rule to Northern Ireland.

A Scottish Parliament is restored to Edinburgh after almost 300 years and a Welsh Assembly is instituted in Cardiff.

1999   cont. A Minimum wage of £3.60 per hour is introduced.

The report into the murder of Stephen Lawrence, a black teenager, declares London's police force is institutionally racist.

The last colliery horse to work underground in a British coal mine is retired.

Dame Iris Murdoch, Irish-born British novelist, dies.

2000   The Millennium Dome and the London Eye open to mark the new millennium.

The Tate Modern museum of modern and contemporary art opens.

Production of the original mini car concept at Oxford ends.

The National Botanic Garden of Wales opens.

Sir John Gielgud and Sir Alec Guinness, distinguished actors, die.

2001   9/11 - the twin-tower Trade Center is destroyed in New York. 67 UK nationals killed.

Sir Timothy Hunt and Sir Roy Nurse are awarded the Nobel Prize in Medicine.

V. S. Naipaul, native of Trinidad, Oxford-educated, wins the Nobel Prize in Literature.

George Harrison, ex-Beatles musician/songwriter, dies.

The Real IRA bombs the BBC TV Centre in White City.

2002   The Golden Jubilee of Queen Elizabeth II.

Queen Elizabeth the Queen Mother dies aged 101.

The Ford Motor Co. ends British car production at Dagenham.

Longannet, Fife, last Scottish coal mine, closes.

2003   Mass protest by 2 million in London as UK troops prepare to invade Iraq, intent on removing weapons of mass destruction and regime change.

England wins the Rugby Union World Cup.

Twenty20 professional game is introduced by the England and Wales Cricket Board.

2004   The Higher Education Act introduces variable tuition fees for University students.

Civil Partnership Act grants the same legal rights to same-sex couples as normal married couples.

Anglo-Canadian Lennox Lewis retires as the undisputed heavyweight champion for all four world boxing organisations.

The Gherkin building designed by Norman Foster and partners opens in the City of London.

The Scottish Parliament building opens in Edinburgh.

John Peel, influential radio presenter and DJ, dies.

2005   Four coordinated terror bombings are set off by Islamic terrorists in London.

A new Prevention of Terrorism Act is passed.

The IRA declared an end to its militarised campaign.

The Prince of Wales marries Camilla Parker-Bowles.

The Hunting Act which bans hunting with hounds or dogs comes into force.

MG Rover, the last British-owned car manufacturer goes into receivership.

Harold Pinter wins the Nobel Prize in Literature.

2006   Final payment of the American post-war loan granted in 1946.

2007   A power-sharing Executive is formed in the Northern Ireland Assembly.

The SNP (Scottish Nationalist Party) leader Alex Salmond becomes First Minister in the Scottish Parliament.

2007   cont. Gordon Brown replaces Tony Blair as Prime Minister.

A run on the Northern Rock Bank, later nationalised by the government, signals financial problems in the UK banking system.

The Treaty of Lisbon introduces constitutional changes to the operation of the EU and recognises the right of a state to leave the union.

A smoking ban is introduced throughout the UK, one year after first being implemented in Scotland.

The rebuilt Wembley stadium opens.

2008   The failure of Lehmann Brothers bank in United States intensifies the global financial crisis.

The British government puts £500 billion into a bank rescue package which involved buying shares in major banks including HBOS, RBS and Lloyds.

Tower colliery, the last deep mine in South Wales, closes.

Woolworths and MFI close all their UK stores.

Humphrey Lyttleton, jazz musician/broadcaster dies.

2009   Bank Rate is reduced to its lowest ever level 1.5% and then 1% and .5% as the UK enters an era of prolonged economic anxiety.

Unemployment rises to almost 2.5million (8.5% of the workforce).

The Bank of England introduces Quantitative Easing as a stimulus for the economy.

The Chilcot Inquiry into British involvement in the 2nd Iraq War begins.

The Speaker of the House of Commons, Michael Martin, resigns after Daily Telegraph publishes details of MPs' expenses abuses.

Hilary Mantel publishes Wolf Hall, first part of her trilogy about Thomas Cromwell.

2009   cont. Harry Patch, the last British survivor of the Great War, dies aged 111.

2010   General Election produces a 'hung parliament'.
        David Cameron forms a coalition Conservative/Liberal Democrat government.
        Chancellor of the Exchequer George Osborne announces severe cuts in public spending.
        Ed Milliband beats his brother David to become the Labour party leader.

2011   Queen Elizabeth II makes a state visit to Ireland.
        Nigel Farage becomes leader of UKIP for second time.
        A referendum rejects the Lib Dem proposal for an Alternative Voting System.
        The UK population increases by 470,000 in the year 2010/11 and census figures record growth of 4.1million or nearly 7% since 2001.
        Shale gas resources are discovered in Lancashire.
        News of the World newspaper closes after 168 years following phone hacking allegations.

2012   The Summer Olympics are held in London for the third time. Team GB finishes third in the medals table.
        The UK National Debt exceeds £1 trillion.
        Unemployment begins to fall from nearly 2.7 million.
        Sex abuse allegations are made about Sir Jimmy Savile, TV personality and charity fund raiser who died 2011.

2013   Same Sex marriage is legalised in England and Wales.
        Moody's downgrades British credit rating from AAA.
        All former Scottish police forces merge into Police Scotland.
        Street parties in ex mining areas mark the semi-state funeral of Margaret Thatcher.
        Islamic terrorism is renewed with the slaughter of Drummer Lee Rigby.

2013   cont. Peter Higgs is awarded the Nobel Prize in physics for the Higgs-Boson particle theory.

Andy Murray is the first British man to win the Wimbledon Men's Singles title since 1936.

Sir Alec Ferguson retires after 27 years as manager of Manchester United.

Alan Turing, wartime codebreaker and computer pioneer at Bletchley Park, is given a posthumous Royal pardon for homosexuality conviction.

Elaine Morgan, feminist and author of The Aquatic Ape and Descent of Woman dies.

2014   Scottish Independence is rejected in a Referendum.

UKIP wins 27% of votes in the European Elections, more than any other British party.

Malala Yousafzai, female/ human rights activist brought to Britain for surgery after being shot in her Pakistani homeland, becomes the youngest winner of the Nobel Prize for Peace.

Kate Bush, influential singer/song writer, performs first live shows since 1979 at the Hammersmith Apollo.

The Invictus Games for wounded service personnel are launched by Prince Harry.

An Independent Inquiry concludes at least 1400 children in Rotherham were subject to sexual abuse 1997-2013. One of several similar events in other areas.

888,245 ceramic poppies art installation at the Tower of London commemorate the centenary of the Great War (WWI).

Nicola Sturgeon becomes the Scottish First Minister.

Libby Lane becomes the first C of E woman bishop (of Stockport).

2015   Conservatives win a small outright majority in the General Election, Scottish Nationalists are completely dominant in Scotland. Liberal Democrats MPs severely reduced.

2015   cont. The Consumer Price Index falls to a record minus .1%.

Queen Elizabeth II becomes Britain's longest serving monarch.

Kellingley colliery, Yorkshire. is closed – end of deep pit coal mining in Britain.

2016   David Cameron renegotiates some aspects of British membership of the EU.

UK Referendum results in vote to leave the EU (Brexit) by 51.9 - 48.1%. Cameron resigns.

Theresa May forms a new Conservative government.

Labour MPs vote no confidence in the leadership of Jeremy Corbyn but he remains as Labour party leader.

The Chilcot Inquiry into the Iraq War criticises govern-ment procedures and decisions leading into the 2nd Iraq war.

18. British Monarchs,

Wales was never a Kingdom but consisted of various principalities until in 1301 Edward I began the custom whereby the English monarch's eldest son was invested as the Prince of Wales.

Ireland consisted of petty kingdoms until Henry II was recognised as Lord of Ireland under Papal authority by Irish leaders in 1171. This continued until 1542 when the Pope's role was ended and the King of England became Ireland's monarch until southern Ireland became independent as Eire in 1937.

Rulers of England

Anglo-Saxons/ Danish

927	Athelstan of Wessex and Mercia
939 Oct.	Edmund I
946 May	Eadred
955 Nov.	Eadwig
959 Oct.	Edgar I
975 Jly.	Edward 'The Martyr' killed at Corfe.
978 Mar.	Ethelred 'the Unready'
1013 Sept.	Sweyn Forkbeard of Denmark acknowledged as king of all England until he died Feb. 1014. Ethelred then resumed his reign.
1016 April	Edmund II 'Ironside'
1016 Nov.	Cnut also king of Denmark and Norway died 1035.
1037	Harold I 'Harefoot' is proclaimed king.
1040 June	Harthacnut
1042 June	Edward 'The Confessor'
1066 Jan. 23	Harold II killed at Hastings 14 Oct.

Normans
1066 Dec. 25   William I 'The Conqueror'
1087 Sept. 26   William II 'Rufus'
1100 Aug. 5   Henry I
1135 Dec. 22   Stephen of Blois (disputed by Matilda or Maud daughter of Henry I)

Plantagenets
1154 Dec. 19   Henry II
1189 Sept 3   Richard I 'The Lionheart'
1199 May 27   John
1216 Oct. 28   Henry III
1272 Nov. 20   Edward I 'Longshanks'
1307 July 8   Edward II
1327 Jan. 25   Edward III
1377 Jun. 23   Richard II deposed Sept. 1399, murdered Feb. 1400.

Lancastrian/Plantagenets
1399 Sept. 30   Henry IV 'Bolingbroke'
1413 Mar. 13   Henry V
1422 Sept. 1   Henry VI deposed Mar. 1461, restored Oct. 1470, deposed and murdered May 1471.

Yorkist/Plantagenets
1461 Mar. 4   Edward IV
1483 April 9   Edward V deposed 25 June, murdered date unknown.
1483 26 June   Richard III

Tudors
1485 Aug. 22   Henry VII
1509 April 22   Henry VIII
1547 Jan. 28   Edward VI
1543 July 6   Jane Grey deposed July 19
1543 July 19   Mary I
1558 Nov. 17   Elizabeth I

Stuarts

1603 Mar. 24   James I and VI of Scotland

1625 Mar. 27   Charles I executed 30 Jan. 1649

Commonwealth of England Lord Protectors:

1653 Dec. 16   Oliver Cromwell

1658 Sept. 3   Richard Cromwell to 24 May 1659

The Restoration

1660 May 29   Charles II

1685 Feb. 6   James II deposed 1688.

1689 Feb. 13   William III and Mary II (died Dec. 1694) joint monarchy.

1702 Mar. 8   Anne

Hanoverians

1714 Aug. 1   George I

1727 June 11   George II

1760 Oct. 25   George III (subject to Regency of Prince of Wales 1811-20).

1820 Jan. 19   George IV

1830 June 26   William IV

1837 June 10   Victoria

Saxe-Coburg-Gotha

1901 Jan. 22   Edward VII

Windsors

The family name was changed from Saxe Coburg-Gotha in 1917

1910 May 6   George V

1936 Jan. 10   Edward VIII abdicated

1936 Dec. 11   George VI

1952 Feb. 6   Elizabeth II

Rulers of Scotland

Kings of Alba (Pictland and the Scots) a large part of modern eastern and southern Scotland.

843	Kenneth I MacAlpin
858	Donald I
862	Constantine 1
877	Aed
878	Eochaid and Giric
889	Donald II
900	Constantine II
943	Malcolm I
954	Indulf
962	Dub
971	Kenneth II
995	Constantine III
997	Kenneth III

Rulers of the Scots (after the acquisition of Lothian and Strathclyde)

1005 Mar. 25	Malcolm II
1034 Nov. 25	Duncan I murdered by Macbeth
1040 Aug. 14	Macbeth killed by Malcolm
1057 Aug. 15	Lulach. Macbeth's stepson killed by Malcolm
1058 Mar. 17	Malcolm III
1093 Nov. 13	Donalbane deposed, restored and finally deposed
1097 October	Edgar
1107 Jan. 8	Alexander I
1124 April 25	David I
1153 May 24	Malcolm IV the Maiden
1165 Dec. 9	William the Lion
1214 Dec. 4	Alexander II
1249 July 8	Alexander III
1286 Mar. 19	Margaret the Maid of Norway died on voyage to Scotland

The First Interregnum 1290-2
1292 Nov. 17 John Balliol (chosen by Edward I of England)
      abdicated 1296
The Second Interregnum 1296-1306. The throne is claimed
by Edward I of England
1306 Mar. 25 Robert I the Bruce
1329 June 7 David II
Period of Strife 1332-57 in which the crown was
claimed by Edward Balliol son of John Balliol, backed by
Edward III of England, and David II was held captive in
England 1346-57.
1371 Feb. 22 Robert II Stewart or Stuart
1390 April 19 Robert III
1406 April 4   James I
1437 Feb. 21 James II
1460 Aug. 3 James III
1488 June 11 James IV killed at Flodden
1513 Sept. 9 James V aged 1
1542 Dec. 14 Mary aged 6 days, abdicated 1567, executed
      in England 1687
1567 Jly 24 James VI became James I of England 1603

Thenceforward England, Wales, Scotland and Ireland
were ruled by the same monarch until Eire became
independent in 1937.

19. Notable Royal Spouses, Mistresses, Favourites and Lovers

Queen Eleanor of Aquitaine (1122 – 1204), was divorced by the King of France before marrying Henry Count of Anjou (who became Henry II of England) when he was nineteen and she was thirty years of age. They had eight children but theirs was a famously tempestuous relationship.

Fair Rosamond Clifford (circa 1146 – 1176), Beautiful young mistress to Henry II. The affair possibly started when Queen Eleanor was pregnant with her last child, Prince John. It was rumoured that the queen poisoned Rosamond.

Queen Isabel of Angouleme (circa 1188 – 1246) was aged no more than twelve when she became the second wife of King John in 1200 by whom she had five children. Her father had already betrothed her to a powerful French noble and, because of this marriage, all John's Norman/Angevin lands were claimed and eventually taken by the King of France. After John's death, Isabella married the son of her first suitor, by whom she had nine more children.

Queen Eleanor of Castile (1241-1290), wife of Edward I. Their marriage was a true love match. When she died at Harby, Nottinghamshire, in 1290 her body was transported to be buried in Westminster Abbey, London. Edward caused eleven Eleanor Crosses to be built, marking each place where the body rested overnight. Three crosses still stand today.

Queen Isabella, the She Wolf of France, (1295 – 1358) daughter of the King of France and wife of Edward II. The marriage was tainted by Edward's homosexual relationships with his favourites and Isabella, aided by her lover Roger Mortimer, deposed and murdered him. Later, her son executed Mortimer but did not punish his mother.

Piers Gaveston (circa 1284 – 1306), favourite of Edward II originated from Gascony. His intimate and expensive relationship with the king excited the enmity of the English nobility who captured him following his return from the last of several exiles and killed him.

Hugh de Despenser, the younger, (circa 1286 – 1326) succeeded Gaveston as the king's favourite. He and the king became deeply unpopular due to their rapacious rule. Despenser was eventually captured and executed by Queen Isabella who, in alliance with nobles led by her lover Roger Mortimer, deposed her husband.

Katherine Swynford (1350 -1403) was mistress and later the third wife of John of Gaunt, Duke of Lancaster, son of Edward III and father to Henry IV by his first marriage. The Tudor royal family traced their ancestry back to this couple.

Queen Margaret of Anjou (1430 -1482) wife of Henry VI. At times, because of her husband's feeblemindedness, she became virtual ruler of England and leader of the Lancastrian cause. Her opposition to the regency of the Duke of York during one of Henry's bouts of insanity provoked the opening disputes between the two houses which led to the Wars of the Roses and the violent deaths of her husband and only son.

Queen Elizabeth Woodville (1437 – 1492) was a great beauty from a family of the minor nobility. It was rumoured that she ensnared her second husband, King Edward IV, with witch-craft. Her husband was succeeded on the throne by his brother, Richard III, who put her two sons by Edward in the Tower of London and seized the crown for himself. However, her daughter Elizabeth married Henry Tudor after he defeated King Richard in battle, thus joining together the houses of Lancaster and York and strengthening the Tudor claim to the throne.

Anne Boleyn circa 1501 -1536) must be mentioned here although there is no room for Henry VIII's other loves and wives. Henry fell in love with Anne at the time when his first wife Katherine was clearly not going to bear him a son. The Pope would not grant Henry a divorce and this caused him to break with Rome and start the English Reformation. He married Anne and they had a child who became England's great queen Elizabeth I. However, after 2 stillbirths, Henry thought the marriage was cursed and he had Anne executed for adultery and witchcraft.

Robert Dudley, Earl of Leicester (1532 – 1588) was in all probability the one true love of Elizabeth I's life. However, she was known as the virgin queen and, although it is unlikely the affair was completely consummated, he remained her closest confidant from her accession until his death.

Robert Devereux, Earl of Essex (1566- - 1601) was the son by her first marriage of Lettice Knollys, second wife of Robert Dudley (see above). He was ambitious and handsome and made the most of his connections in the aging Elizabeth's court. His arrogance and incompetence led him to try the Queen's patience beyond hope of repair and he then led a half-cocked rebellion, for which there was only one sentence - death by beheading.

George Villiers (1592 - 1628), favourite and likely lover of James I was born a commoner and was created Duke of Buckingham, which provoked the enmity of Parliament and the nobility. At the king's death he was already a close friend of the new king, Charles I. His continued association with numerous foreign policy disasters led to his murder.

Nell Gwynne (1650 – 1687) is the best-known and remembered of Charles II's many mistresses. Her early career - selling oranges in Drury Lane - and her natural wit helped her command the affection of the common people – a rare compliment for royal mistresses.

Sarah Churchill nee Jennings (1660 – 1744) was Queen Anne's closest friend from well before her accession to the throne until their final quarrel in 1710. When Anne became queen their friendship enabled Sarah to gain vital political support for her husband, John Churchill, Duke of Marlborough. Even after losing the queen's friendship, Sarah continued to be a serious political force into the early Hanoverian era.

Mrs Maria Fitzherbert (1756 – 1837) was a twice married widow when she attracted the attention of the Prince of Wales, later to become George IV. She was a Catholic and resisted the prince until he enticed her into an illegal form of marriage in 1785. She acted as his wife and hostess at Brighton Pavilion until he renounced her in 1794 in preparation for his disastrous marriage to Caroline of Brunswick. The relationship was renewed in 1800 until 1807 when the prince took another mistress. She was always respected and treated well by his royal brothers.

Lord Melbourne (1779 – 1848) was prime minister when Victoria came to the throne aged 18. He was her political mentor and confidante in the early years of the reign, which was a time of social and political change with the Whig and Tory party identities becoming outmoded.

Albert, the Prince Consort (1819 – 1861), took over from Melbourne the role of chief advisor and supporter to the queen. They became grandparents to nearly all the European ruling houses and partly due to him the moral, academic and intellectual life of the country was revitalised. His death was an almost unsupportable blow to the queen.

It is well known that Victoria and Albert's eldest son and heir, Edward, Prince of Wales later Edward VII, had many mistresses but none did anything or was of sufficient importance to national life to warrant an entry here.

Mrs Wallis Simpson (1896 -1986) the twice divorced American woman for whom Edward VIII precipitated a national crisis by abdicating the throne in 1936, leaving his ill-prepared brother to take the crown. They lived abroad for the rest of their lives as Duke and Duchess of Windsor, subject to rumours that they had contemplated a return to Britain should Nazi Germany win the war.

Diana, Princess of Wales (1961 – 1997) was involved in an ill-matched marriage with the heir to the throne. Highly popular with the media and public, she supported a wide range of charities and good causes. Their divorce, shortly followed by her tragic death, caused a major trauma in the life and popularity of the queen and royal family which now appears to be improved by public approbation for their grown sons and the queen's steadfast attention to duty.

20. Noteworthy Prime Ministers

Sir Robert Walpole, a Whig, is regarded as the first Prime Minister. It is not possible to give absolute dates for Walpole's ministry because he dominated parliament from about 1721 -1742 without always holding a senior appointment, but he is undoubtedly the longest serving British Prime Minister due to his great political and management skills. He survived the accession of George II, who had been at odds with his father, because he was a close friend of the new Queen Caroline. Walpole is credited with safeguarding the develop-ment of the Hanoverian dynasty and the principles of the Glorious Revolution.

William Pitt the elder, first Earl of Chatham, was prime minister from 30 July 1766 – 14 Oct 1768 but nearly all his greatest achievements were secured when he was the informal leader of the government from 1756 - 61. He was a brilliant orator and was admired for his financial probity. His leadership during the Seven Years War helped secure the victories which gained an empire and led to British dominance in world affairs. He argued it was unconstitutional to impose taxation upon American colonists but he became crippled by physical and mental ill-health and collapsed in the House of Lords arguing against granting independence for the American colonies. He died a few days later at home in 1778.

Lord North was prime minister for George III, with whom he had a friendly relationship, 1770 – 1782. His ministry passed the acts which led to the War of American Independence. He was aware that he was an unsuitable war leader and frequently offered to resign but the king dissuaded him. He was eventually forced out by political adversaries as the war drew to an end.

William Pitt the younger became Tory prime minister at the age of 24 in 1783. He retained the office until 1801 but returned in 1804 and died in office in 1806 aged 46. In his early days in Parliament he supported making peace with the American colonists and other liberal causes such as parliamentary reform. He was a friend of Wilberforce, the anti-slavery spokesman, but on attaining power his first concern was to restore the public finances (he introduced Income Tax and simplified customs and excise duties). He shared the alarm and fear of revolutionary ideas from France which spread throughout the British ruling class in the 1790s and supported repressive measures including suspension of Habeas Corpus, but he felt compelled to resign when George III refused to accept Catholic emancipation as a companion piece to the Act of Union with Ireland. He was recalled to power but died in office, living long enough to see Napoleon's triumphs at Ulm and Austerlitz and Nelson's at Trafalgar.

Spencer Perceval was Tory prime minister from 1809 until his death on 11 May 1812 when he was shot in the lobby of the House of Commons by John Bellingham. To date, no other prime minister has been assassinated. Perceval helped his War Secretary, Lord Liverpool, fight off attempts to recall Wellesley's expeditionary force from the Iberian Peninsula in 1810 thus enabling Wellesley to drain the French resources in Spain before driving them out of the country in 1813.

Lord Liverpool, Tory prime minister (8 June 1812 – 9 April 1827) for the entire Regency period and beyond, led a powerful team which ensured the political and financial support which brought military success for Wellesley in Spain and saw off the challenge from the United States in the War of 1812. In the difficult post-war years his government was vilified for allowing passage of the Corn Laws, which kept the price of bread high, and harsh repression of political expression such as the Luddite riots. However he spoke for the abolition of the Slave Trade and supported the repeal of the Combination Acts. He resigned when the cabinet expressed support for Catholic emancipation.

Duke of Wellington, the national war hero, was Tory prime minister (22 Jan 1828 – 16 Nov 1830 and again briefly at the end of 1834) for short and relatively undistinguished periods of time. Despite his extremely conservative nature, Wellington's administration passed the act giving Catholics political emancipation, despite public hostility. Wellington fought a duel with an opponent of the bill, Lord Winchelsea. Faced with mounting unpopularity the Duke resigned but he continued to serve in subordinate positions in Peel's ministry.

Earl Grey, Whig prime minister 22 Nov 1830 - 16 July 1834. This brief period saw two great landmarks in British history. The passing of the Great Reform Act of 1832 modestly increased the number of electors and, more importantly, corrected the abuse of rotten and pocket boroughs, by which many seats in the Commons were tightly controlled by a few wealthy patrons. The Abolition of Slavery throughout the British Empire was the final act in the long anti-slavery campaign started by Granville Sharp in 1772. Earl Grey tea is named after this man.

Sir Robert Peel, prime minister 10 Dec 1834 – 8 April 1835 and 30 Aug 1841 – 29 June 1846, was born outside the aristocratic magic circle – his father was a wealthy northern textile manufacturer. Before becoming prime minister he had already achieved much in the field of politics; he reformed the criminal law, established a police force and he was also in the forefront of the burgeoning Free Trade movement. His first brief term of office achieved nothing. The second was beset by the tragedy of the Irish Potato Famine and he sought Whig support to ensure the Corn Laws were repealed. This split the old Tory party and left the Peelite wing eventually to merge with liberal Whigs into the Liberal Party. For at least ten years there was confusion in the ranks of Parliament about true party beliefs.

Lord Palmerston was twice Liberal prime minister separated by a brief Conservative ministry (6 Feb 1855 – 20 Feb 1858, 18 June 1859 – 29 Oct 1865). The second administration ending with his death at the age of 81. His consuming interest was foreign affairs with which he had been involved for many years in previous Whig administrations but, during his spell as Home Secretary he oversaw some socially progressive legislation. He was distrusted by the queen and many political colleagues but the electorate admired his nationalist commitment and he was adept at maintaining a balance of power in Europe to Britain's advantage. He was the last prime minister to die in office.

Benjamin Disraeli, Earl of Beaconsfield, was the leading minister in three short-lived administrations headed by the Earl of Derby, briefly became prime minister in 1876 before leading a Conservative administration (20 Feb. 1874 – 23 Aril 1880). He led the country landowners who split with Peel over the Corn Laws and was instrumental in forming the new Conservative party, a remarkable achievement considering he was born a Jew and was a novelist. He was quite progressive in Home affairs and proved skilful in looking after British interests abroad. His rivalry with Gladstone and his friendly relationship with Queen Victoria is well-known.

William Ewart Gladstone was the longest serving of Victoria's prime ministers, but he never enjoyed her affection. His political career began as a Peelite member of the Tory party. As Chancellor of the Exchequer in Liberal ministries, he introduced many of the Free Trade measures which underpinned British prosperity through-out most that period. In his later periods as prime minister he proposed a number of radical measures, especially Home Rule for Ireland, which split the Liberal party. He was prime minister on four separate occasions (3 Dec 1868 – 20 Feb 1874, 23 April 1880 – 23 June 1885, 1 Feb – 25 July 1886 and 15 Aug 1892 – 5 Mar 1894).

The Marquess of Salisbury served as Conservative prime minister late in Victoria's reign (briefly in 1885, 25 July 1886 - 15 Aug 1892, 25 June 1895 -12 July 1902) and was in power when she died. He was deeply conservative in temperament as well as politically and led the Unionist opposition to Irish Home Rule. However, his first ministry brought in an act which permitted working class housing to be improved with the aid of public money. In his early years he travelled the Empire, forming a good opinion of many of the peoples therein, except the South African Boers, with whom Britain went to war during his last premiership.

Herbert H. Asquith was the last prime minister to form a Liberal government (5 April 1908 – 5 Dec 1916). The 'People's Budget' of 1909 was bitterly opposed by the House of Lords. Although they eventually accepted the budget, the power of the Lords was curtailed by the Parliament Act of 1911. Asquith formed a coalition government after war broke out in 1914 but he proved an indecisive war leader and was eventually forced to retire.

David Lloyd George known as the Welsh Wizard was a great orator and energetic social reformer. He became prime minister (5 Dec 1916 – 19 Oct 1922) of a coalition government and was regarded as an outstanding war-time minister and premier. The coalition won a massive majority in 1918 but his popularity waned with scandals attached to his name, especially rumours that he had sold honours. When his Conservative partners left the coalition, he remained a controversial figure and the Liberal party, under his leadership, found much of its support ebbing away to the Labour and Conservative parties.

Ramsey MacDonald was the first Labour party prime minister. He led minority Governments (22 Jan – 4 Nov 1924 and 5 Jun 1929 - 1931). The economic challenges of the Great Depression caused him to form a coalition government with

Conservative support (24 Aug 1931 -7 June 1935) and he was consequently expelled from the Labour party. However the coalition won an enormous mandate in the 1931 election and MacDonald battled increasing bad health to lead the government for four more years.

Stanley Baldwin became prime minister briefly (23 May 1923 – 16 Jan 1924) but resigned when he failed to gain an outright majority in the general election. He returned to power (4 Nov 1924 – 5 June 1929). His government faced down the General Strike and passed an act for universal female suffrage. He joined MacDonald's coalition in 1931, became P M once more (7 June 1935 – 28 May 1937) and had to deal with the abdication crisis.

Baldwin's policies were continued by his successor Neville Chamberlain who will be remembered for the appeasement of Hitler at Munich in 1938 and his broadcast announcement that Britain was at war with Germany 3 Sept 1939. He failed to gain the confidence of the House of Commons regarding war policy and resigned after an expeditionary force was driven out of Norway by the Germans in 1940.

Sir Winston Churchill, wartime prime minister (10 May 1940 – 26 July 1945) and again 26 Oct 1951 – 6 April 1955). His long and uneven political career reached its zenith with his warnings about Nazi Germany in the 1930s and the wartime speeches in which he inspired the nation to stand alone against Hitler. In 1951 he led the Conservative party to its first majority administration since 1924 - 1929 and, despite suffering a stroke, he held office until he was aged eighty. His over-riding interest was foreign policy but his peacetime government accepted the social reforms of Attlee's administration, abolished the last of the rationing system but struggled to redress the dire post-war economic situation.

Clement Attlee, prime minister (26 July 1945 – 26 Oct 1951), led the Labour party to a landslide victory after the war. His administration will always be associated with policies to implement the Beveridge Plan such as the National Health Service. It ended the British Raj in India with a handover of power to nations on the subcontinent and introduced a nationalisation programme which brought Railways, Coal, Steel and other industries into government ownership. The administration always struggled with financial problems, devalued the pound and became split over introducing prescription charges in the NHS.

Harold Macmillan succeeded Sir Anthony Eden, whose administration (1955 – 1957) ended due to Eden's ill-health following the debacle of the Suez invasion. Macmillan was Conservative prime minister (10 Jan 1957 – 19 Oct 1963). He was known as Supermac and continued with the post-war mixed economy established by Attlee, but he also encouraged the growth of a consumer society to boost an aura of prosperity with low unemployment – hence his phrase 'you've never had it so good'. He continued with the dissolution of empire and rebuilt a special relationship with Kennedy's USA. Towards the end of his time the Profumo affair rocked the government and he resigned in favour of the Earl of Home who had to renounce his title and take a seat as Sir Alec Douglas Home in the House of Commons before he could accept the office of P M (1963 – 1964).

Harold Wilson, prime minister (16 Oct 1964 – 19 June 1970, 4 Mar 1974 – 5 April 1976), gained power with a promise to remake Britain in the 'white-hot heat of the technological revolution'. The balance of payments became an increasing problem in his first period of office and the pound was again devalued in an attempt to overcome the problem. He came back to power with a small majority in the 'who governs Britain' election to face industrial relations problems and a worsening economy. He called the referendum which confirmed the UK as a member of the EEC. His government also introduced comprehensive education.

Edward Heath won a surprise election victory and became Conservative prime minister (19 June 1970 – 4 Mar 1974). After nursing the policy in previous Conservative administrations, he finally achieved the UK's entry into the European Economic Community (EEC) or Common Market as it was known. He intended to bring in a measure of economic deregulation but was overwhelmed by an inflationary spiral and seriously bad industrial relations, ending with cuts in the supply of power and the imposition of a three day working week. His time as P M ended with failure to win the 'who governs Britain' election.

James Callaghan became P M following Wilson's abrupt resignation and remained in power through the agency of the Lib-lab Pact with the Liberal party 5 April 1976 – 4 May 1979. Remembered mainly for putting the economy under the supervision of the World Monetary Fund and worsening industrial relations in the 'winter of discontent'.

Margaret Thatcher, first woman prime minister (4 May 1979 – 28 Nov 1990). She ended the post war consensus with monetarist and free market policies of deregulation, trades union reform, privatisation of nationalised industries and reform of practises in the City of London. Her 'Thatcherite' agenda brought her into conflict with 'one nation' Con-servative colleagues, but after the Falklands War she won the party's support, despite mounting unemployment and widespread closure of businesses which accompanied her economic policies. She earned admiration for her bravery when she addressed the party conference hours after narrowly avoiding death when the Grand Hotel at Brighton was blown up by the IRA in 1984, but formidable political opposition continued with the miners' strike of 1984-5. She won three consecutive general elections and became a close ally of President Reagan. Known as 'The Iron Lady', she was widely regarded overseas as a major player in the downfall of the Soviet Empire. Her Bruges speech opposing the formation of a federal Europe and growing unpopularity of her 'Poll Tax' policy at home led to a party revolt and her resignation. She was afforded the honour of a semi-state funeral at St Paul's cathedral on her death in 2013 but remained a divisive figure to the end.

John Major, prime minister (28 Nov 1990 – 2 May 1997) became beset by problems caused by moves to federalise the EEC. His policy of tying the £ to the Deutchmark at an unfavourable exchange rate collapsed when it was forced out of the European Exchange Rate Mechanism on 'Black Wednesday' 16 Sept 1992. This led to a period of UK economic growth but the government became de-stabilised by Conservative eurosceptic opposition to the terms of the Maastricht treaty which brought the European Union (EU) into being, despite Major achieving opt outs from the Currency Union and the Social Chapter. His cabinet escaped unscathed when the IRA fired a mortar bomb at Downing Street. However, following an IRA ceasefire, he began the Northern Ireland Peace Process which led to the Good Friday Agreement.

Tony Blair, is, to date, Labour's longest serving prime minister (2 May 1997 – 27 June 2007) winning three consecutive victories under the 'New Labour' emblem. His administration passed important constitutional changes including reform of the House of Lords (without solving the problem of how members were to be selected), the Belfast agreement which brought in a power-sharing government for Northern Ireland, a devolved parliament for Scotland and a devolved Welsh National Assembly. Many social changes were also enacted. Public expenditure was greatly increased, aided by so-called stealth taxes, increased borrowing and other, off-book, financing methods. Immigration numbers, including an influx of people from the new East European members of the EU, grew significantly during this period. Blair eventually came under fire from many in his party because of the way he presented to Parliament and the country the case for going to war with Iraq.

Blair's position was under regular challenge from the Chancellor of the Exchequer Gordon Brown who eventually succeeded him in 2007, only to be confronted by the world-wide Economic Depression in 2007-8 which wrecked the economy and led to the partial nationalisation of Bank of Scotland and other British banks. Brown belatedly signed the Lisbon Treaty which promoted ever closer union in the EU and he was defeated in the general election of 2010.

David Cameron became Conservative leader of a coalition government in partnership with the Liberal Democrats (11 May 2010 – 7 May 2015). The immediate task was to deal with the serious economic situation, which led to measures to reduce government borrowing, serious cuts in most public services and a large increase in student tuition fees. Interest rates fell to a record low of .5% for a record period of time and employment figures unexpectedly improved. A referen-dum in Scotland as to whether the country should become independent of the UK resulted in 55.3% rejecting the proposal.

After an unexpected victory in the 2015 election, Cameron formed a Conservative government (7 May 2015 – 13 July 2016). Following a renegotiation of membership terms with Brussels, a referendum was held in June 1916 to decide whether the UK should remain in or out of the EU. A 52.8% majority voted in favour of leaving. Cameron promptly resigned and Mrs Theresa May formed a government later that summer

INDEX

Athelstan, King of the English 927

Attenborough, Sir David 1979

Attlee, Clement 1945

Augustine, Saint 597

Austen, Jane 1817

Australia 1700, 1768, 1788, 1901

Austria 1193

Awdry, W. Rev. 1949

Axis powers 1941, 1942

B

BBC, TV service 1936, 1961, 1967, 1969, 1988

BBC, TV Centre 2001

BBC, radio 1949, 1951, 1954

Baden-Powell, Lord 1907

Bakewell, Robert 1783

Balfour Declaration 1917

Ball, John 1381

Ballot, Secret first 1872

Bank Holiday, first 1871

Bank of England 1694, 1780, 1946, 1997, 2009

Bank Rate 2009

Bank Rescue Package 2008

Bannister, Sir Roger 1954

Bannockburn, battle of 1314

Barbados 1625, 1966

Barings, merchant bank 1995

Barnardo, Dr. Thomas and Orphanage 1870

Barrows, Long c3500 BCE

Barrows, Round c1500 BCE

Barry, Sir Charles 1840

Bart, Lionel 1960

Baylis, Lilian 1931

Bazalgette, Joseph 1858

Beatles, the 1963, 1980, 2001

Becket, Archbishop Thomas 1170

Bede, the Venerable 731

Beecham, Sir Thomas 1932

Beeching Report, the 1963

Belgium 1914

Belle Vue, Manchester, greyhound track 1926

Belsen, Concentration Camp 1945

Bengal 1757

Bennett, Alan 1960, 1988

Bentham, Jeremy 1832

Bentinck Lord William 1829

Berkeley Castle 1327

Berlin Airlift 1948

Berlin Wall 1990

Bermuda 1609

Berners-Lee, Sir Tim 1989

Betjeman, Sir John 1972

Bevan, Aneurin 1948

Beveridge Report 1942

Beyond the Fringe 1960

Bible, Authorised Version 1610

Big Bang, financial reorganisation 1986

Bill of Rights, the 1689

Bismarck, German battleship 1941

Black Death, the 1349

Black Prince, Edward the 1356

Black Wednesday 1992

Blair, Tony 1994, 1997, 2007

Church of England, women priests 1992

Churchill, John Duke of Marlborough 1704

Churchill, Winston Sir 1933, 1940, 1946, 1951, 1965

Circulation of Blood, theory 1619

Civil Partnership Act 2004

Civilisation, TV documentary 1969

Clare, John poet 1864

Clark, Lord Kenneth 1969

Clarkson, Thomas 1807

Claudius Emperor 43

Clean Air Act 1956

Clive, Robert 1757

Cnut, King of all England 1016

Coal Mines, nationalisation 1947

Coalbrookdale 1709

Coalition Government 2010

Cockroft, John 1932

Cobbett, William 1802

Coinage Reform 1486

Coke, Sir Edward 1610

Colchester 43 AD, 61

Coleridge, Samuel Taylor 1798

Colliery horses 1999

Collins, Canon John 1958

Collins, Michael 1922

Colne, cinema 1908

Colour TV service 1967

Columba, Saint 563

Combination Act 1799, 1824

Comedy Playhouse TV series 1961

Comet jet airliner 1949

Common Market (EEC) 1967, 1973

Common Pleas, Court of 1610

Common Prayer, Book of 1549

Commons Enclosures 1830

Commons, House of 1642, 1950, 1979, 1989, 1992, 2009

Commons Protestation, the 1621

Commonwealth Immigration Act 1962, 1968

Commonwealth of England 1649

Commonwealth of Nations 1949, 1989

Commonwealth War Graves Commission 1960

Community Charge 1989

Communist Party of Great Britain 1920

Comprehensive Education 1965

Concorde, supersonic aircraft 1969

Conrad, Joseph 1924

Conscription 1916

Conservative party 1834, 1846

Constable, John 1837

Constantius, Emperor 296

Constantine the Great, Emperor 306

Consumer Price Index 2015

Convicts, First Fleet 1788

Conwy 1283

Cook, James Captain 1768

Cook, Peter 1960

Cooperative, first shop 1844

Coram, Thomas 1739

Corbyn, Jeremy 2016

Golf, British Open Championship 1860
Golf, rules of 1744
Good Friday Agreement 1998
Goon Show, radio comedy 1949
Gorbachev, Mikhail 1984
Gordon, General Charles George 1885
Gordon Riots, the 1780
Grahame, Kenneth 1908
Grand Alliance, the 1701
Grand National 1839
Great Anarchy, the 1154
Great Britain, steamship 1843
Great Exhibition, the 1851
Great Reform Act 1832
Great Stink, the 1858
Great Train Robbery, the 1963
Great War, the 1914, 1918
Greene, Graham 1950, 1991
Greenham Common 1981
Greenwich 1884
Greenwich Mean Time 1847
Greer, Germaine 1970
Gregorian Calendar 1752
Gregory I, Pope 597
Grenville, Sir Richard 1591
Gresham, Sir Thomas 1571
Grey, Lady Jane 1554
Guinness, Sir Alec 2000
Gulliver's Travels 1726 amended 1735
Gunpowder Plot 1605

H
H4 Chronometer 1759

Habeas Corpus 1640, 1679
Hadrian, Emperor and Wall 122
Hall, Sir Peter 1961, 1973
Hammersmith Apollo, theatre 2014
Hampden, John 1636
Handel, George Frederick 1743
Hangings, Public 1868
Hanover, George Ludwig Elector of 1714
Hardy, Kier 1893
Hardy, Thomas 1928
Hargreaves, James 1764
Harold II, King 1066
Harrison, George 2001
Harrison, Joseph 1759
Harry, Prince 2014
Harvey, William 1619
Hastings, battle of 1066
Hastings, Warren 1784
Hawkins, Sir John 1562-4
Health & Morals of Apprentices Act 1802
Health, Board of 1848
Heaney, Seamus 1995
Hengist 430
Henley Regatta 1839
Henry I, King 1100
Henry II, King 1154, 1170, 1174, 1171
Henry III, King 1258
Henry V, King 1415
Henry VI, King 1455, 1471
Henry Tudor VII, King 1485
Henry VIII, King 1533, 1534
Henry, Prince of Wales 1501

Irish Republican Army (IRA) 1917, 1922, 1970, 1979, 1984, 1987, 1991, 2005
Irish Republican Brotherhood 1858, 1867, 1913
Irish Volunteers 1913
Iron Curtain speech at Fulton, Missouri 1946
Ironbridge 1781
Isabella, Queen 1327
Islamic Cultural Centre 1977
Islamic Terrorism 2005, 2013
Israel 1948
Issigonis, Alec 1959
Italy 1941

J

Jack the Ripper 1888
Jacobite Rebellion 1715, 1745
Jallianwalla Bagh massacre 1919
Jamaica 1655, 1865
James I & VI of Scotland, King 1603
James II, King 1685, 1688, 1690
James IV, King of Scotland 1513
James, Naomi 1978
Jamestown, Virginia 1607
Japan 1941
Jarrow March, the 1936
Jarrow, monastery 731
Jeeves 1919
Jeffreys, Judge 1685
Jenner, Edward 1796
Jerusalem 1191
Jerusalem, song and poem 1808

Jesus Christ Superstar, musical 1972
Jet propulsion engine 1937
Jewish Homeland 1917
Jews, expulsion of 1290
Jews return of 1655
Joan of Arc 1432
Jockey Club 1750
John, Prince 1193, King 1215
John II, King of France 1356
Johnson, Doctor Samuel 1755
Jones, Brian 1969
Julian Calendar 1752
Julius Caesar 54 BCE
Jungle Book the 1894
Jutes circa 447-50
Jutland, battle of 1916

K

Kabul, retreat from 1841
Kapital Das 1867
Kean, Edmund 1814
Keble, John 1833
Kellingley Colliery 2015
Kenneth MacAlpin, King of Scotland 843
Kenya 1952, 1964, 1968
Kent 430
Keynes, John Maynard 1930
Khartoum 1885, 1898
King David Hotel, Jerusalem 1946
Kingdom of Great Britain 1707
Kipling, Rudyard 1894
Kitchener, Lord 1915
Kitchener's Army 1916

London, first underground tube service 1863
Londonderry 1972
Longannet, coal mine 2002
Lord Chamberlain 1968
Lord of the Flies, the 1954
Lord Protector 1653
Lord, Thomas 1814
Lords cricket ground 1814, 1962
Louis XIV, King of France 1701
Lucan, Lord 1974
Luddite outbreak 1811
Lyric Ballads 1798
Lyttleton, Humphrey 2008

M
MI Motorway 1959
MCC, the 1787
MCC, bodyline tour 1933
MG Rover, motor company 2005
MPs, expenses abuse 2009
Maastricht, Treaty of 1993
Macauley, Thomas Babington 1838
Macbeth, King of Scots 1040
Macdonald clan 1692
Macintosh, Cameron 1986
Mackintosh, Charles Rennie 1897
Macleod, Ian 1970
Macmillan, Harold 1957, 1960
Magna Carta 1215
Maiden Castle c 3500 BCE
Malaria 1902
Malay Federation, the 1957
Malaya 1941, 1949

Maldon, battle of 991
Malta 1942, 1971
Manchester United FC 1958, 2013
Mandela, Nelson 1990, 1995
Mansfield, Lord Chief Justice 1772
Mantel, Hilary 2009
Marconi, Guglielmo 1901
Marian Martyrs 1553
Marie Rose, warship 1545, 1982
Marine Insurance 1690
Married Women's Property Act 1870
Martin, Michael 2009
Marx, Karl 1867, 1883
Mary, Queen of Scots 1559, 1567, 1587
Mary of Guise 1559
Mary I, Queen 1553, 1554
Mary II, Queen 1689
Marylebone Cricket Club (MCC) 1787
Matilda, the Empress 1154
Matthews, Sir Stanley 1965
Mau Mau 1952
Maximus, Emperor 388
May, Theresa 2016
Mayflower, the 1620
Maze Prison, Belfast 1981
McLean, Donald 1951
Merchant Shipping Act 1876
Mercia 655, 784, 927
Messiah, Hallelujah Chorus 1743
Meteorological Office, the 1854
Methodist Conference, the 1784

Metrication Board, the 1968
Metropolitan Police Act 1829
MFI stores 2008
MI5 counter espionage 1909
Military Service Act 1916
Mill, John Stuart 1873
Millais, John E. 1848
Millennium Dome 2000
Miller, Jonathan 1960
Milliband, David 2010
Milliband, Ed 2010
Milne, A. A. 1926
Milton, John 1667
Miners' Strike 1984, 1985
Mines Act 1842
Mini Car 1959, 2000
Minimum Wage, the 1999
Missolonghi, Greece 1824
Mitchell, R. J. 1936
Moghul Emperor, the 1690
Monasteries, Dissolution of 1536-9
Montagu, Lord 1983
Montfort, Simon de 1258, 1265
Montgomery, Viscount Field Marshal 1942, 1945
Moody's credit rating agency 2013
Moore, Dudley 1960
Moors Murders trial 1966
More, Sir Thomas 1535
Morgan, Elaine 2013
Morris, William 1896
Mortimer, Roger 1327
Moscow, Treaty of 1990
Mosley, Sir Oswald 1932

Mount Badon, battle of 516
Mountbatten, Earl 1979
Mousetrap The, play 1952
Munich air crash 1958
Murdock, Iris 1999
Murdoch, Rupert 1986
Murphy Catherine 1789
Murray, Andy 2013
Murray, James 1884

N
NATO 1949
NSPCC 1889
Naipaul, V. S. 2001
Nanking, Treaty of 1842
Nantes, Edict of 1685
Naseby, battle of 1645
National Debt, the 2012
National Front, the 1967
National Gallery, the 1824
National Health Service (NHS) 1948
National Heritage Collection, the 1983
National Insurance Scheme 1911
National Playing Fields Association, the 1933
National Portrait Gallery, the 1859
National Service, Conscription 1960
National Theatre Company, the 1963, 1973
National Trust, the 1895
Nationalisation 1946, 1947, 2007
Navigation Acts 1660

Printed in Great Britain
by Amazon